GW01418606

A Systematic C
Project Management

A modern, multi-disciplinary and community-centric perspective

by

Ken Thompson

and

Paul Hookham

June 2018
REVISION: 1.02

A Systematic Guide to Project Management

Except as provided by the Copyright Act 1968, no part of this publication may be reproduced, stored in any retrieval system or transmitted in any form or by any means without the prior written permission of the authors.

All rights reserved.

Table of Contents

About the Authors

Ken Thompson is an expert practitioner, author and speaker on collaboration, high performing teams, change management, game-based learning, experiential learning and social learning.

Ken's work has featured in major publications including The Guardian Newspaper, Wired Magazine, The Huffington Post and The Henry Ford Magazine.

Ken has also spoken at many international events including TEDx, the Institute for Healthcare Improvement (IHI), Learn Tech (London) and NASA.

Paul Hookham is a highly experienced and successful business and IT delivery executive with an outstanding track record of success, working for some of the world's most demanding customers.

Paul is passionate about quality and believes that people do their greatest work in an empowered, blame-free, supportive and learning environment.

Paul is also a Master Practitioner of Neuro-Linguistic Programming (NLP), an NLP Master Coach, a published author and experienced speaker.

<u>Reviews of the Systematic Guide Series</u>

"Systematic Guides" are little Gems. Here we have another precious gift for the world of business and organisations. This is essentially a practical guide and a perfect companion to several of Ken's Business Simulations. It would prove helpful to novices as well as expert practitioners, as it creates a powerful scaffolding to hang whatever little or extensive knowledge the reader may already have."

DR. JUAN PEREZ-CAMACHO
Faculty Emeritus at Intel Corporation and Programme Designer at the Irish Management Institute

As an athlete in Team GB, I spent years working as a squad then forming crews to race at the Olympic level. We would compete for our places in the team then come together and collaborate to beat the real opposition in international competition. In any team, it's vital to have real conversations to understand each other's beliefs and motivations. Ken's book will help you focus on what really matters so you can drive Olympic level performance whilst maintaining healthy relationships.

GREG SEARLE MBE
Olympic Gold and Bronze medallist. Executive Coach and Consultant to individuals, teams and organisations.

I work with a number of high performance teams and find Ken Thompson's book very helpful. What I particularly like is the way I can open it anywhere and remind myself of vital aspects of team interaction.

PROFESSOR ALISTAIR FEE
Co-Founder Squid Academy

We have used the simulations in Ken's book to provide us with a significant extra dimension to our training offer by combining technology, experiential and immersive learning in an accessible package. The book introduces the theory behind these simulations and is invaluable reading for facilitators and training professionals who want to successfully introduce Game-Based Learning to their clients.

MARK PALMER
Managing Director, OEE Consulting. Turning business strategy into operational reality.

Ken has written a succinct yet powerful summary of change management thinking, approaches and tools, presented in a practical and accessible manner. Excellent reading for anyone involved with the leadership and management of change.

CHRIS COLLISON
Author and Former Director of Change and Knowledge Management, Centrica.

Although Ken Thompson brilliantly and quickly summarizes the best of the best change-management thinkers, John Kotter, Robert Kaplan and David Norton, Jeannie Daniel Duck, Robert H. Schaffer and Harvey A. Thomson, and Mark Hughes, this book is no simple epitome of the best thinking in change management. Ken Thompson is changing change management. He is one of the leading-edge practitioner-thinkers who is carefully evolving change management from a planning discipline into a political one.

CHARLES SPINOSA, Ph.D.
Group Director & Leader, Strategy and Customer Experience VISION Consulting

<u>The Systematic Guides" Series</u>

This volume is the 6th book in "The Systematic Guides" Series also featuring:

VOLUME 1: A Systematic Guide to High Performing Teams (HPTs), Ken Thompson, December 2015

VOLUME 2: A Systematic Guide to Game-Based Learning (GBL) in Organisational Teams, Ken Thompson, January 2016

VOLUME 3: A Systematic Guide to Business Acumen and Leadership using Dilemmas, Ken Thompson, February 2016

VOLUME 4: A Systematic Guide to Change Management, Ken Thompson, July 2016

VOLUME 5: A Systematic Guide to Collaboration and Competition within Organisations, Ken Thompson, March 2017

All books are available on <u>Amazon</u> and make ideal delegate briefing notes for participants in game-based learning sessions by providing the underpinning theory and supporting best practice on each key topic.

Why did we write this book?

It is impossible not to read about the constant stream of high profile technology project failures in areas such as travel, banking and healthcare. Sadly, these seem to have progressed beyond just inconveniencing people or damaging their finances, to costing their lives.

We also constantly read about an industry that seems fixated with certifications, agility, awards and quality. But how can an industry with such a worthy focus keep getting it so badly wrong?

We seem to have somehow lost the essence of what is required to manage and deliver any non-trivial project - we call it "The Stool of trusted delivery" and it's not complicated!

Which Project Management "Stool" should you trust?

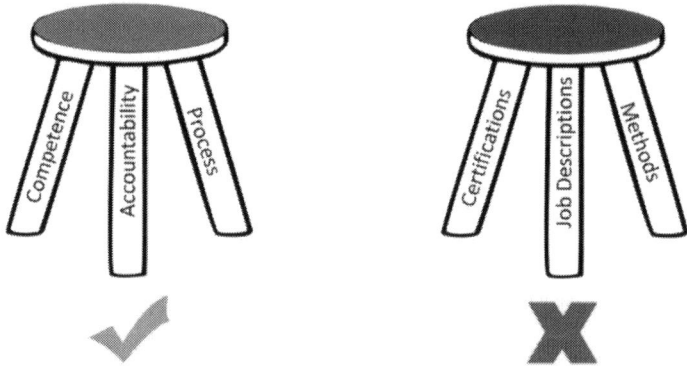

The trust stool has three legs and like any three-legged stool, if one of these legs is broken then the stool can be turned upside down and used as a bird table but is of no use to anybody as a seat.

The 3 legs of the trust stool are:

1. Competence
2. Accountability
3. Process

You need all three legs to consistently deliver anything important - if any single one of them is missing you will fail.

There are three common failure scenarios in the stool:

#1 Lack of competence or experience

Would you fly with a pilot who is self-taught on Microsoft Flight Simulator? Some key certifications in project management today can be achieved in under a week with no prior experience!

#2 Lack of accountability

Without clear accountability structures it won't work and it will be nobody's fault and nothing will be learned. Successful projects are delivered on the back of solid commitments and not just allocated responsibilities!

#3 Lack of due process

If due process is missing, then sometimes it will work but mostly it won't. The fail will usually occur when there is a bit of unexpected pressure. There is an important concept known as "Process Fidelity." The best process in the world is of no value if it's not used consistently by the whole team. Likewise, a simple and short process can be of great value <u>provided</u> it is appropriate, understood and consistently applied.

These days it seems some organisations are constructing what looks to us like "false trust stools". The three legs of such a stool look a bit like this:

1. Certifications and Training
2. Job Descriptions and Work Plans
3. Methods and Techniques

These organizations and their leaders seem to be sleep-walking into a classic category error - confusing evidence for something for the thing itself.

Training and certifications are evidences of a person potentially having a particular skill at a given level. However, these are only two of many different potential evidences, including interview performance, past project narratives and independent endorsements. All of these available evidences need to be ranked, probed and assessed to be able to form a good judgement of whether a person does in fact possess a skill at the level required.

If we can go back to basics, with the triangle of trusted delivery, then there is really no reason and no excuse for these technology project failures to keep on happening. It is not complicated, but it is difficult, time consuming and costly - and definitely not a 'quick fix'.

One of our main driving forces behind writing this book, is to try to get back to the basics of good project management. Our goal is to try to pull together a concise summary of everything a project manager NEEDS to know and nothing that they don't!

Ken Thompson
Paul Hookham
June 2018

Introduction & Executive Summary

If you ask a business or technical person to define what the essence of Project Management is "off the top of their heads", they will probably suggest that it is about planning and executing various tasks, in a pre-defined order to achieve a specific goal.

If you probed a bit further about the "goal aspect", they might say it requires the creation of certain "deliverables" which are needed to achieve certain "outcomes". (In reality, these outcomes are usually far from certain though few will admit it).

This is probably as far as most people would go in their elevator pitch for "What do I mean by Project Management?"

In one sense, these interpretations are fundamentally correct as no project will succeed without planning, deliverables and outcomes. However, in another sense such interpretations totally miss the point of Project Management – possibly because of the perspective they fall into – that of a project manager.

This popular interpretation has huge pitfalls which have their most extreme manifestations in large projects that may well be completed on time and within budget but are totally unfit for purpose. All the tasks may have been completed on time and within budget, but they are the wrong tasks. All the deliverables may have been signed off according to strict acceptance criteria, but they are the wrong deliverables.

Aha – you may say, I think I know what's missing – they have neglected Change Management!

Good spot! However, just like the Project Managers, you would also be correct but still missing the point. Of course, Change Management is needed to lay the foundations for all the people, structural and process changes that are needed for a project to achieve its objectives. However, if the project is still framed from the Project Manager's mindset, all that Change Management will achieve is to make it fail more elegantly but with a much wider group of people to share the blame with than before.

What about Agile Project Management I hear you cry?

Surely Agile is the missing ingredient with its short review cycles and integrated project teams. This would surely stop deliverables being created which were only discovered to be useless after the fact? Again, you would be right to say this - it is very important, but the weakness of Agile (like any other ways of working) is that it often becomes an end in itself in terms of its methods and processes and sucks up people's attention and energy from more important things.

So, if it's not Change Management and it's not Agile then what is the missing ingredient in the currently popular interpretation of Project Management?

The mention of a Project Manager's "perspective" and the term "management" within Project (and Change) Management are clues. Different perspectives and the need for management suggest that there is a "we" element of Project Management which is mostly underplayed.

If you have the Project Management mindset of producing artefacts, you will never get the "we" aspect of project management or at best you will just get the limited project manager's perspective of who the "we" are.

The argument in this book is that the essence of project management is to "produce useful transformations within a community of sponsors, users (and deliverers)".

If you do not have this interpretation at the forefront of your mind when you are managing or participating in projects, then your success will be limited at best and disastrous at worst.

You simply can't deliver a successful project by coming up with a detailed work breakdown structure <u>before</u> any work has started and when the requirements are at their most vague, though many sponsors still insist upon it. All that happens is that the project team respond by protecting themselves via a 'Victorian-novel' change control process.

Back in 2008, in his book - "Bioteams", Ken explored the lessons that can be drawn from nature about how to organize teams more effectively – organisational biomimicry to use its full name! In the book, he coined 12 rules for organising our teams more effectively.
Rule number 10 (Self-Organising Networks) stated that "teams should define themselves in terms of network transformations - not outputs."

"Biological processes often require a catalyst (or enzyme) to be present, to enable and accelerate the required chemical transformations – the same applies in organisational teams. The key point here is that each bioteam goal and role should be primarily defined in terms of what other living network components it transforms, not in terms of inanimate objects".

That is what we are talking about here – that the essence of project management is creating useful transformations with communities (or networks).

But what do we mean by transforming a community?

We define Community Transformations as "behavioural (and often attitude) changes within a target segment of community members normally linked by having common roles." To achieve such transformations, we usually need to make something possible, easier or more beneficial for the target group.

To cite a simple banking example: "possible" could be that customers are now able to view their account balances online whereas before they had to ring up; "easier" could be that customers don't have to hold on in a telephone queue for so long and "more beneficial" could be that customers now earn more interest on their current account balances.

One massive word of caution here: -

Having the community mindset is "necessary but not sufficient for success" as our mathematics teachers were very fond of saying. You still need all the Project Planning, the Change Management, the short review cycles and the integrated teams. But these activities need to be subservient to an overall community transformation perspective which is at the heart of everything done in the name of the project.

Who are these communities?

Firstly, there is the **Leadership Community** – with two main roles that its members play in a project:
- *Sponsors* - who authorise and invest in projects on behalf of the organisation.
- *Stakeholders* - who have an interest in projects and are vital to their success.

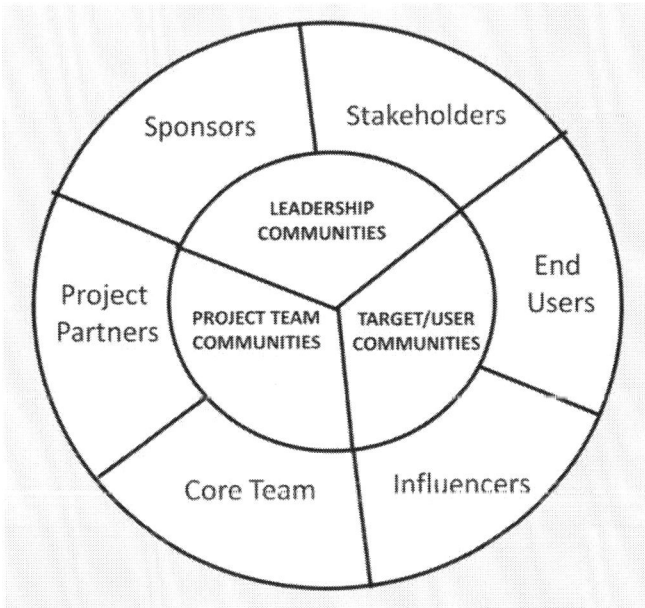

Figure 1 – Project Management Communities

Secondly, there are the **Target Communities** – also with two main roles that its members play in a project:

- *Influencers* – those who have strong reputations and social networks.
- *End Users* – those whose work will be impacted by the project.

These are the two primary communities that manifest useful transformations from the project. However, there is also a third community, without which no transformations can happen - the Project Team Community.
Important transformations, such as team member development, need to occur within this community to enable transformations in the other two communities.

The **Project Team Community** also has two main roles that its members play on a project:

- *Core Team Members* - whose work on the project is directly controlled by the Project Manager
- *Project Partners* - whose help the project manager needs but does <u>not</u> control

In some projects, all communities would be internal to the organisation whilst in other projects, there might be both internal and external components. Note also that communities can have multiple segments with which to engage.

For example, target communities for a major project to refurbish a hotel would be both internal staff (and other project partners such as external subcontractors) and external customers (and prospective customers). The transformations in the external community would have a dependence (necessary but not sufficient) on the transformations in the internal community

In the chapters that follow, we will flesh out 12 key disciplines of Project Management from the community perspective. We will suggest that each of these three communities require four key project management disciplines to achieve valuable community transformations.

The astute reader might have noticed the word "Multi-Disciplinary" adjective in the book title. We believe that once you begin to look at project management through the lens of communities then the multi-disciplinary nature of the job becomes extremely clear.

Figure 2 below breaks down the role of a Project Manager into 24 "jobs" spread across the three communities and six sub-communities.

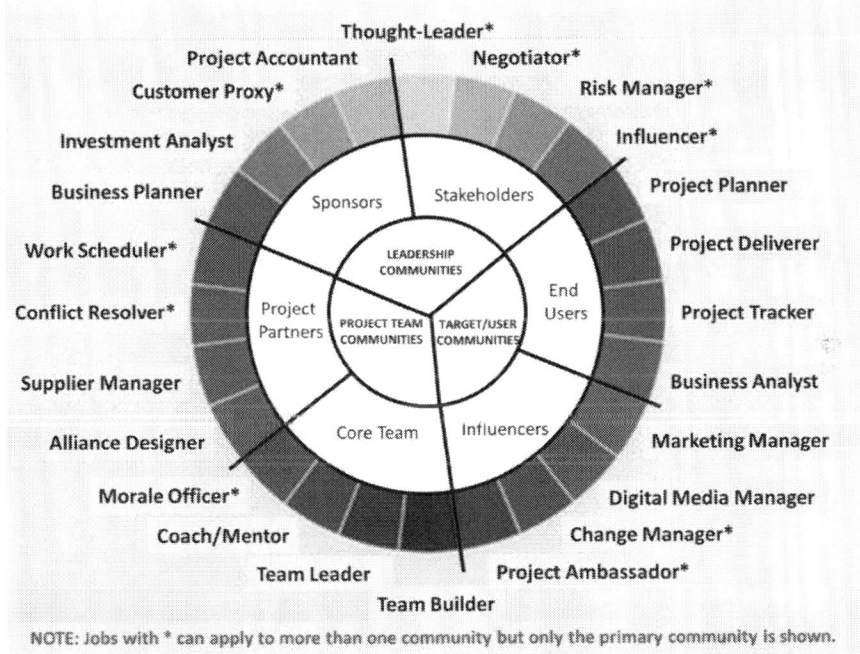

NOTE: Jobs with * can apply to more than one community but only the primary community is shown.

Figure 2 – 24 Project Manager Jobs

Readers should therefore appreciate, in a fresh way, the truly multi-disciplinary nature of project management "in its entirety". An effective Project Manager might need to quickly take on any of the jobs in the diagram (Figure 2), as needs dictate.

Project Managers performing their roles in this manner truly deserve and earn our respect. Depending on your perspective, Project Management can be a truly enormous job!

In Figure 3, you will see all of the usual candidates for best practices in project management, such as Business Plans and Team Work Allocation, but described using the new lens of community. You will also encounter some other practices, such as User Adoption and Partner Engagement, which you might not normally expect to find in a book on Project Management but which, from the community perspective, also turn out to be crucial ingredients for success.

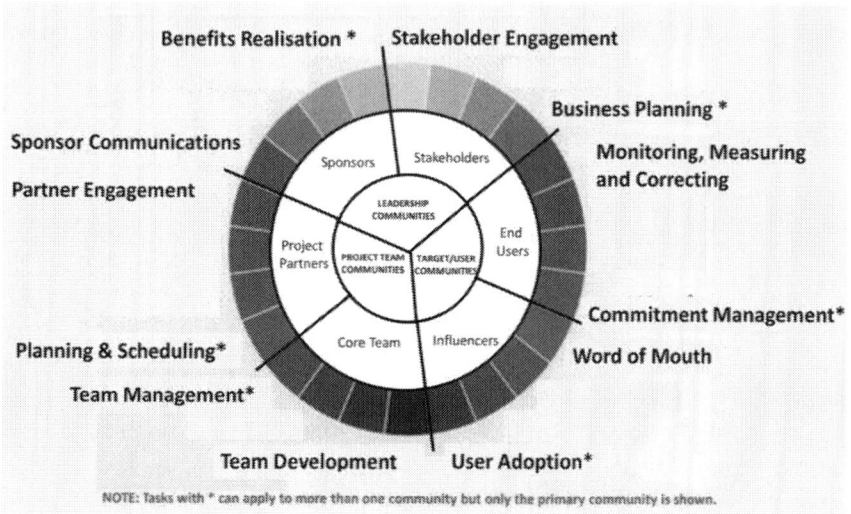

NOTE: Tasks with * can apply to more than one community but only the primary community is shown.

Figure 3 – 12 Project Management Tasks

Another word of caution – *Albert Einstein* is quoted as saying "All models are wrong - but some are useful". Many of these 12 tasks (those marked with *) impact more than one community although they are shown, for simplicity, against just one.

Finally, the authors are firm believers in the value of using business simulations to allow learners to make the project management mistakes, which are essential for real learning, in environments with are both safe personally and in terms of adverse business consequences.

We have therefore included chapters on the rationale for, and use of, business simulations to practice and improve different project management skills. We include a reference at the end of each chapter to a current project management-related simulation and a final chapter (Chapter 14) with a short description of the six specific simulations.

1. Business Planning

<u>Primary Focus</u>
Primarily Leadership Communities but also Target Communities.

<u>Key Objectives</u>
Assessing realistic project timeframes, costs, benefits and risks.

<u>Key Chapter Topics:</u>
- Project Business Cases
- Business Case Calculations
- Community Transformations and Agile Stories
- Project Indicators and Measures
- Leading and Lagging Indicators
- Project Risk Assessment
- Dealing with Uncertainty
- Confidence Intervals
- The Delphi Technique: Collective Judgement
- Example Team Simulation

1.1 Project Business Cases

The purpose of a Business Case is to estimate the costs and the benefits of a proposed project with the different options (including do nothing) and their associated risks.

According to *'The Business Case Checklist'* by Business Case Pro, which is an excellent, short 48-page booklet and a good investment in itself, there are 12 key questions you should consider when making a major investment, often with a technology aspect to it:

1. What is the business need?
2. What is the investment that addresses the business need?
3. What technology underlies the investment?
4. What are the benefits of the investment?
5. What are the costs of the investment?
6. What are the major risks?
7. How did we value the investment?
8. Is the investment feasible and a good fit?
9. What alternatives did we consider?
10. How do we execute on the investment?
11. Is this a good business case?
12. Do we invest?

Each of these 12 topics can be broken down into a number of sub-questions, for example:

1. *What is the business need?*
- Is the business need clear and understood?
- Is the business need acute?
- What is the complication which makes the status quo unbearable?
- Why solve this problem now?

Surprisingly, however, the checklist above does not ask the obvious question 'What Change Management will be required?'

1.2 Business Case Calculations

There are a handful of different calculations usually associated with Business Cases. The terminology can be quite daunting to the non-mathematical but, in essence, they are quite straightforward and common sense.

The most common calculations are:

Net Benefits: the total benefits <u>less</u> the total costs to achieve those benefits.

Return on Investment (RoI): the ratio of the net benefits to the total costs expressed as a percentage.

Payback (or Break Even) Period: the time taken for the total benefits gained to become equal to the total costs invested.

Net Present Value (NPV): an investment calculation which discounts by an annual rate to consider the reality that money tomorrow is less valuable than money today. Also known as **Discounted Cash Flow (DCF).**

Internal Rate of Return (IRR): is the annual discount rate which would make the NPV equal to zero. Effectively, the bank interest you would need to earn to match your project return.

Please note that if you do need to use NPV or IRR, be careful to base your final decision on NPV not IRR. IRR is easier to understand and good for discussion but does not give you the absolute value and does not account for the number of years for which the return is earned.

<u>*A simple worked example*</u>

Imagine we invest £100 in Year 0 and get £50 back each year for 3 years, then:

Net Benefits = (3* £50) - £100 = £50

Return on Investment (RoI) = 100 * (£50/£100) = 50%

Payback (or Break Even) Period = 2 Years

Net Present Value (NPV):
At an annual discount rate of 8%
PV (Present Value) = $50/(1.08)^1 + 50/(1.08)^2 + 50/(1.08)^3$
= £129
NPV = £129 - £100 = £29

Note the difference between the Net Benefits and the NPV!

Internal Rate of Return (IRR):

The annual discount rate which would make the NPV equal to zero – in this case it's about 23%. Note the actual calculation requires an IRR calculator (there are many available free on-line and on traditional calculators).

CAPEX versus OPEX expenditure

One other distinction which needs to be understood in preparing (and reading) business cases is the difference between Capital Expenses (CAPEX) and Operating Expenses (OPEX). CAPEX are typically large one-off expenses which appear on your Balance Sheet as assets which are subject to depreciation. OPEX are typically smaller recurring expenses which appear on your Profit and Loss and are not subject to depreciation.

1.3 Community Transformations and Agile Stories

One of the biggest challenges in Business Planning is coming up with a compelling but realistic narrative about what it is you want the project to achieve.

One of the most common pitfalls is to describe what it is you want to do rather than what it is you wish to achieve.

In our introductory chapter, we talked about the importance of not viewing a project as a set of outputs but rather a set of transformations within the target and other communities. We gave a simple banking example which hinted that there were at least three main types of transformation within a community or group:

- *Possible*: enable something to happen which was not previously possible

- *Easier*: make something which was difficult - easier

- *Better*: make something which has to be done better (e.g. cheaper or quicker)

Agile Stories (aka Use Cases) are a simple technique used by software developers to quickly and concisely get to the heart of what is needed for an IT System.

We propose that Agile Stories can be adopted and adapted to define the high-level outcome narrative needed in a business case. The recommended format of an agile story is very simple:

As a (role) I want (something) so that (benefit).....

For example, Figure 1.1 shows typical Agile Stories from a Virtual Communities Project run by Sei-Mani (www.sei-mani.com):

Agile Story Examples (Virtual Communities Project)

As the business owner of a customer provisioning system, I want to create a community so that we can share hints, tips and best practice across a user community of 1,000 users.

As a loyalty planning and performance analyst, I want to create a community so I can gauge wide scale opinions across the business quicker and more easily.

As a head of department, I want to create a community so that I can share information "verbally" reducing the need to use email, which risks not being read.

As a Telemarketing Manager, I want to create a community so that I can see the quality of opportunity being created for Field Sales (12 agents, 1-2 opportunities a day).

As a Sales Manager, I want to create a community so I can quickly be able to react to customer sales queries and be able to enhance the customer experience.

As a channel development manager, I want to create a community so that our external facing social media team can get super fast resolution to the customer issues which are raised.

Source: www.sei-mani.com

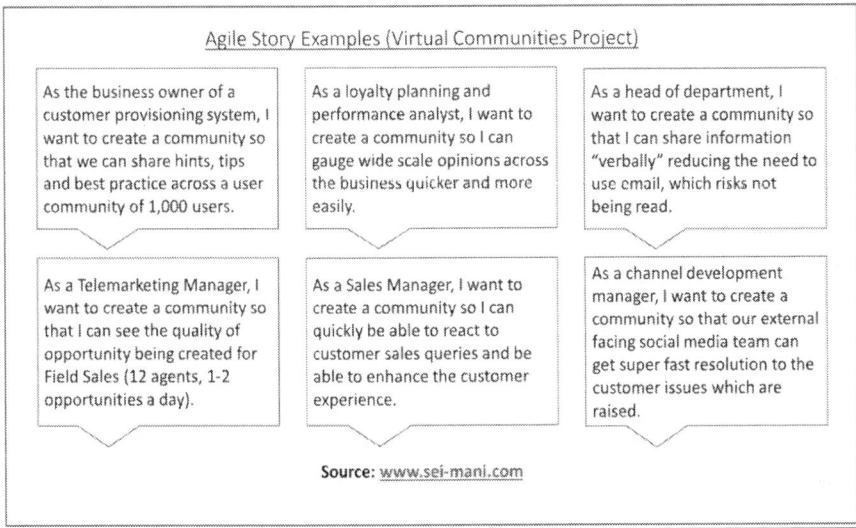

Figure 1.1 – Agile Stories

Let's take one of these and develop it a bit further for our purposes:

As a training manager, I want to create a learning community so I can share videos, FAQs and my recorded classroom sessions so that people can consume knowledge at their own pace and also collaborate with experts if they have questions.

Note the key elements of the story – the role, the want (something) and the "so that" (benefit).

We can extend the standard agile story in two ways to make it more useful by adding:

... and I will be confident that it is going to succeed if (results/measures).

.... and I will know it was a good return on investment if (results/measures).

Our example story could now become:

As a training manager, I want to create a learning community so I can share videos, FAQs and my recorded classroom sessions so that people can consume knowledge at their own pace and also collaborate with experts if they have questions.

I will be confident that it is going to succeed *if 10 new videos are shared each month and 100 videos are viewed and* **I will know it was a good investment** *if at least 80% of my community assessed it has helped them learn valuable new skills AND 80% of their end-users have observed an overall improvement in their skill levels.*

Note that "Confidence" is looking forwards on the basis of certain types of early warning measures known as Leading Indicators and "Return on Investment" is based on looking backwards based on other kinds of measures known as "Lagging Indicators".

Before we look at these types of indicators in more detail let's summarise.

We propose that the outcomes narrative in a project business case can be very effectively presented as a collection of agile stories for each of the key roles within the target communities of the project.

1.4 Project Indicators and Measures

Without a good set of project indicators, you will have three huge problems that you will not be able to resolve:

- prepare a professional project business case

- effectively track project progress and costs

- conduct any meaningful form of benefits realisation

One of the main challenges you will encounter in project management is deciding which results you should 'steer' by in terms of judging how things are going. There are two main problems – delays and fixation.

Many results, typically financial, happen long after the activity which caused them has ceased. These are referred to as 'lagging' indicators and are *outcome* measures. They are an essential perspective on a business as ultimately profits are what the business is there to generate.

However, because they are lagging indicators, they are not effective early warning indicators because by the time you see them, all the activities which could have influenced them have been completed. Example lagging indicators include Sales, Revenue, Costs and Profits.

Other results, typically non-financial, happen well in advance of the lagging indicators. These are referred to as 'leading' indicators and are *activity* measures. They are also an essential perspective on a business as they provide excellent early warning systems and can allow you to conduct a *Root Cause Analysis* of problems.

However, because they are leading indicators, they are not effective outcome measures and never tell the ultimate story of how a business is doing in a way which would satisfy its investors. Example leading indicators include proposals made per month, exit rates of customers, customer satisfaction levels and employee retention levels.

If you take the analogy of an aircraft pilot - airspeed and estimated time of arrival are lagging indicators whereas engine temperatures, altitude and headings are leading indicators.

One of the most common causes of airplane crashes is called CFiT (Controlled Flight into Terrain) which means that pilots have flown a perfectly good plane into a hillside or the ground. How could this happen?

One of the main reasons is that the pilots spot an issue, typically accompanied by a warning light, and *fixate* on this single issue at the expense of the other critical indicators such as airspeed and altitude.

Malcolm Gladwell discusses the cultural issues around this in his book '*Outliers*'. He dedicates a whole chapter to the concept of 'Power Distance' which inhibits junior pilots from correcting the mistakes of senior pilots in some cultures – even if they are flying the plane into the ground.

Therefore, to successfully manage the results of any project, you need to have a balance of leading and lagging indicators and avoid fixation on any one or two indicators at the expense of the others.

1.5 Leading and Lagging Indicators

The approach outlined here is known as the Balanced Scorecard approach to managing business, developed by Robert Kaplan and David Norton. We will cover it in more detail in Chapter 2 - Benefits Realisation.

1.6 Project Risks

No section on Business Planning would be complete without mentioning Project Risks. In its simplest form your Business Case should identify the main risks associated with each project option. For each risk identified, you need to establish four critical things:

- *Likelihood* - the probability of it happening - typically high, medium or low

- *Impact* - the consequences of it happening - also high, medium or low

- *Mitigation* - what you are doing to ensure it does not happen

- *Backup* plan - what you will do if it does happen

It is quite easy to remember these via the simple acronym - LIMB. You don't ever want to go out on a LIMB in your project business case!

1.7 Dealing with Uncertainty

However, let us not pretend that risk analysis is an exact science as we are dealing with two very challenging concepts – The Future and The Unknown.

What do we know, what are we assuming and what do we not yet know? What can we do to reduce these uncertainties?

"There are known knowns. There are things we know that we know. There are known unknowns. That is to say, there are things that we now know we don't know. But there are also unknown unknowns. There are things we do not know we don't know." - Donald Rumsfeld, US Secretary of State for Defence, 2002.

Although at the time, Rumsfeld was ridiculed by some for talking nonsense, he was making a very important point about knowledge management which we will develop a bit further. There is a simple 2x2 matrix we can construct

(Figure 1.2) to represent the current state of our knowledge of any topic. It has four distinct cells:

	KNOWN	**UNKNOWN**
KNOWN	Known Knowns	Known Unknowns
UNKNOWN	Unknown Knowns	Unknown Unknowns

Figure 1.2 – Knowns vs. Unknowns Matrix

Known Knowns (top left)

What you know you know. The critical and often forgotten action is to **make sure everybody on your team who needs to know also knows**.

Known Unknowns (top right)

What you know you don't know. You can list the headings of the topic areas (e.g. personal relationships between your competitors and your prospective customer) but you don't yet know the answers. You need to prioritise these topics and try to find this out the answers.

Unknown Knowns (bottom left)

What you know but don't know you know. In other words, someone in your community may already have the answer to this but you need to find them. This is the classic problem of organisational memory or rather the lack of it. How do we know what we already know? To address this, you also need to "mine" your existing network for the priority topics you identified under your "known unknowns" to see if some are just "unknown knowns".

Unknown Unknowns (bottom right)

What you don't know you don't know. By definition, you can't purposefully find these out. To address this, you need to be in a mode of constantly looking and listening for new and unexpected information on multiple channels, no matter when it appears and where it comes from.

Not all information is of equal credibility. You also need to assess the quality of each bit of information. For example, you can think of three simple categories of information reliability:

- Definite - you would bet your house on it

- Probable - you would bet a day's wages on it

- Possible - you might risk a bet to buy a colleague a drink on it

For critical information, which is in the lower reliability categories, you will need to do further investigative work to promote it up to a higher category. Also, note that a big element of information reliability is currency - it may have been true five years ago, but is it still the case?

1.8 Confidence Intervals

In the early stage of a project, you will have to deal with uncertainty. In fact, at all stages of a project you deal in uncertainty. To create business cases and estimates, we need to be precise in the numbers we select. However, we must not make the fatal mistake of confusing "precision" with "accuracy".

One practical technique for quantifying uncertainty is "Confidence Intervals" which is well articulated in the excellent book "How to Measure Anything" by Douglas W. Hubbard.

Let's take a simple example

If I am 90% confident that my team will score at least one goal and not more than six goals in their next game, then my 90% confidence interval for this question is one - six. Sounds simple!

However, research shows that almost everyone systematically over-estimates or under-estimates their confidence levels unless they are "calibrated". In fact, from experience, most people err on the side of over-optimism!

Calibration

So how do you start "calibrating" as a group - it's not as painful as it sounds! You first need to help your group become aware of the problem.

All you need is a short five-minute quiz with just ten questions, each of which requires the group members to estimate 90% Confidence Intervals. For example, one question could be "what is your 90% confidence level for when England won their only soccer World Cup?" Your colleagues guess the lower and upper boundaries (e.g., 1946 and 1996 respectively) and if the right answer (1966) is inside these boundaries, then they get a tick for being correct. If not, they get an X for being wrong. At the end of the quiz everyone calculates their scores - they should be all getting around 90%, because you asked for their 90% Confidence Interval!

However, surprise surprise - 50% (five questions right or less) is usually much closer to the average team result.

You can build your questionnaire in advance or even on the fly by taking two minutes to have everybody contribute a question, with a numeric answer which they know the exact answer to, and which the other team members would not know exactly but should be able to make a good guess at.

People sometimes say their poor score is not a reflection on whether they are optimistic or pessimistic about their estimates and commitments but really they just didn't know the answer to those specific questions.

This is a common fallacy. Think about it!

If you have little idea of the answer, then you should just make your 90% confidence interval really wide.

Note- don't let people choose absurdly wide intervals as these are not 90% confidence intervals – they are 100% confidence intervals!

Now that you have shown your colleagues their natural tendencies to be overly optimistic (or in some cases overly pessimistic) then you can go straight to the job in hand – reviewing and agreeing various estimates on costs, returns, timescales and risks for the project.

You then need to use the space you have created for everyone to challenge each other when they smell a bad estimate!

Betting on the business

Another technique which can be employed here is to get everyone to think about making "bets" on their estimates and those of their colleagues. Research shows (and the whole business of prediction markets is based on this) that when you make a bet, your estimates are significantly improved!

So, if you use this very simple technique, you can seriously improve the quality of your project estimates by first showing your colleagues whether they are natural optimists or pessimists in picking numbers.

Another useful way of dealing with uncertainty is Delphi.

1.9 Delphi Technique: Collective Judgement

The Delphi Technique is a proven way to harness collective group intelligence (popularly known as "the wisdom of crowds") in a wide range of applications. It is also non-proprietary and supported by some excellent free resources.

Delphi has been around since the 1950s, with a large body of support material, case studies and on-line tools that should be part of a project manager's toolset.

About 15 years ago, a naive (but enthusiastic) software project manager was first introduced to the Delphi technique to try and produce better software development estimates - an area fraught with failure.

More recently, this very same person has been looking at Delphi again, prompted by James Surowiecki's book – *'Wisdom of Crowds'* and discovered that it is much more than a software estimating technique and has been successfully used for:

- Gathering current and historical data, not widely or accurately known or available
- Examining the significance of historical events
- Evaluating possible budget allocations
- Exploring urban and regional planning options

- Planning university campus and curriculum development
- Putting together the structure of a model
- Delineating the pros and cons associated with potential policy options
- Developing causal relationships in complex economic or social phenomena
- Distinguishing and clarifying real and perceived human motivations
- Exposing priorities of personal values and social goals

History of Delphi

Delphi was born way back in the early 1950s, out of a US Air Force sponsored research study by Rand Corporation. Its objective was to develop a method for "obtaining the most reliable consensus of a group of experts by a series of questionnaires, interspersed with controlled opinion feedback".

There are many different definitions of Delphi but in generic simple terms it can be defined as:

"A method for structuring a group communication process so that the process is effective in allowing a group of individuals, as a whole, to deal with a complex problem"

To accomplish this "structured communication", there are generally four main elements in any Delphi exercise:

1. Feedback of individual contributions of information and knowledge
2. Assessment of the group judgement
3. Opportunity for individuals to revise views
4. Some degree of anonymity for the individual responses

Delphi has a large body of public domain support resources and case studies. One of the best resources is a free e-book on the Delphi Method by Harold Linstone and Murray Turoff, which is drawn on heavily here.

Delphi is applicable to a wide range of group applications, particularly those with the following characteristics:

- The problem does not lend itself to precise analytical techniques but can benefit from subjective judgements on a collective basis
- The individuals needed to contribute to the examination of a broad or complex problem have no history of adequate communication and may represent diverse backgrounds with respect to experience or expertise
- More individuals are needed than can effectively interact in a face-to-face exchange
- Time and cost make frequent group meetings infeasible
- The efficiency of face-to-face meetings can be increased by a supplemental group communication process
- Disagreements among individuals are so severe or politically unpalatable that the communication process must be refereed and/or anonymity assured
- The heterogeneity of the participants must be preserved to assure validity of the results, i.e.,

avoidance of domination by quantity or by strength of personality ("bandwagon effect")

Finally, a word of warning

Because Delphi is so easy to use, Linstone and Turoff report that many people think it is just 'common sense' and try it out without properly understanding it first. These Delphi exercises are inevitably unsuccessful, so it is highly recommended that you review the free resources first and try out the support tools before you unleash it on your unsuspecting organisation, team, community or network.

Example Business Simulation

The PLAY-IT Business Simulation (described in 14.1) allows participants to engage with key Business Case Calculations as they decide which projects to invest in.

2. Benefits Realisation

Primary Focus
Primarily Leadership Communities but also Target Communities.

Key Objectives
Tracking the delivery of financial and non-financial benefits throughout the lifetime of the project from the users' perspective.

Key Chapter Topics
- Balanced Scorecards
- Cause and Effect
- Five Key Measurement Categories
- The Different Types of Measure
- Benefits Realisation Example
- Example Team Simulation

2.1 Balanced Scorecards

The Balanced Scorecard is regarded as one of the best approaches to developing and managing the strategy and has a strong set of empirical evidence of business success.

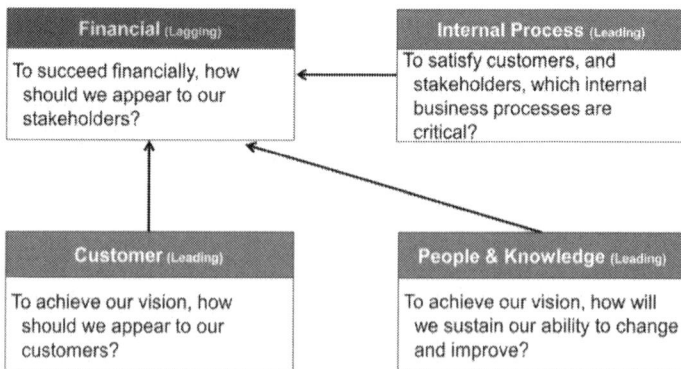

Figure 2.1 - The Balanced Scorecard

The Balanced Scorecard approach suggests that there are four key perspectives that we should measure and track:

1.   Financial

2.   Customer

3.   Process

4.   Learning

The financial perspective is generally a lagging or outcome class of measure which is driven by the other three, which are generally leading indicators.

Balanced Scorecards are constructed by interviewing senior members of the organisation in order to identify candidate indicators. To narrow these indicators down to a practical scorecard, there are various best practices:

- 1 or 2 lagging measures for every strategic objective

- If we have a choice of more than 1 measure, we should use the one that best tracks and communicates the intent

- Not more than 25 measures per scorecard

2.2 Cause and Effect

One of the most important aspects of developing a useful Balanced Scorecard is understanding and defining the relationships between the leading and lagging indicators. In Balanced Scorecard terminology, these relationships are captured as Strategy Maps. Elsewhere, they are also known as Causal Maps, Root Cause Analysis and Cause and Effect Diagrams because they help to differentiate between the visible effects and the often invisible root causes of a situation.

Such maps are immensely valuable because this is one of the biggest challenges you will ever face in business – am I fixing the cause of this problem or merely addressing one of its symptoms? If I fix the cause, the problem should be solved but if I only fix a symptom, the problem will probably keep coming back in different guises.

Let's look at an example Cause and Effect situation.

Imagine an area of a business which is responsible for generating new sales. So, we start on the right-hand side of a blank page recording **SALES REVENUE.**

We then ask ourselves - what causes this? We might say **SALES ORDERS** and **AVERAGE ORDER VALUES.** We record these to the left of **SALES REVENUE.**

We then ask - what causes these two elements? We might decide that **SALES ORDERS** are the effects of **SALES BIDS** (or **SALES PROPOSALS**) and record it to the left. But what causes **AVERAGE ORDER VALUE?** That is a trickier question which we will come back to!

If we continue, we eventually construct a Cause and Effect diagram which might look something like the one in Figure 2.2:

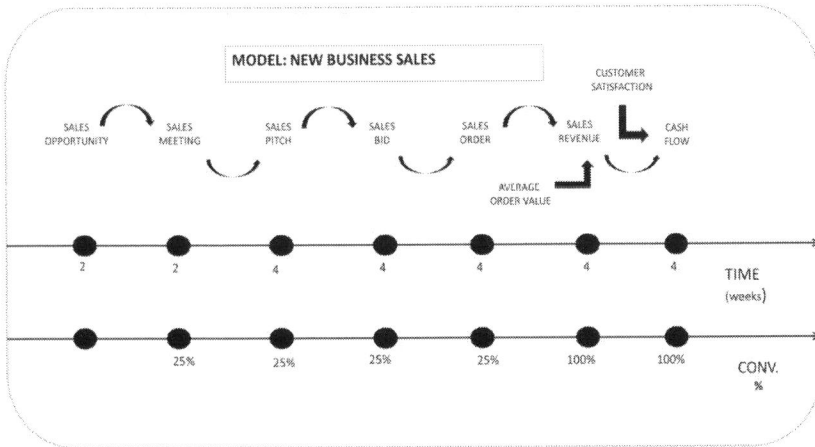

Figure 2.2 – Example Cause and Effect Diagram

But how might this help us?

There are several ways:

Firstly, we now know that if we have a problem with **Sales Revenue** (symptom) then the cause of this could be anything to the left of it on the diagram.

Secondly, if we add the timeline axis, we can see that if a problem occurs in **Sales Opportunities**, it could take 18 weeks before it impacts revenue, so **Sales Revenue** would not be a good early warning indicator of potential problems.

Thirdly, if we add the conversion axis, we can see that to get one new **Sales Order**, we would typically need four **Sales Bids**, each of which would need four **Sales Pitches**, requiring four **Sales Meetings** and four **Sales Opportunities**.

So to get one sale, it would take 4*4*4*4 = **256 Sales Opportunities.**

If our conversion rates are correct and we only have 25 **Sales Opportunities** in our pipeline, then this is a great early warning of another big problem which will show up 16 weeks later in **Sales Revenue**.

Cause and Effect Diagrams are very powerful tools. They also highlight flaws in our thinking about what the real drivers of business results are. Also, in terms of the Balanced Scorecard, Cause and Effect diagrams link financial results to the other perspectives of performance - Customers, Processes and Learning.

In the previous example, we indicated that receiving the actual customer payment will also be dependent on customer satisfaction (not happy = delay payment) which would be a key measure in the Customer Perspective aspect of the scorecard.

In addition, our discussion about the causes of Average Order Values clearly connects to the Learning perspective if we discover that more experienced sales people have the highest order values - and the reasons for it.

Measuring Inputs versus Outputs

However, even with a good balanced scorecard in place for the project, it is still possible to fixate on the wrong measures:

A workable measurement system will address what can be called the "importance versus measurability" dilemma:

"A bad measurement system makes that which is measurable important (typically inputs and outputs). A

good measurement system makes that which is important measurable (normally leading indicators and end results)".

This quote has been applied in the context of the UK Education System and specifically School and University League Tables. However, it applies generally in that there is always a temptation to make what is easy to measure important.

2.3 Measurement Categories

It is useful to identify different categories of measurement and to ensure they are all represented in the project measurement scoreboard. The five categories shown in Figure 2.3 should also be considered:

Measurement Category	Category Example (in the context of a collaboration project)
Type 0 INPUTS	Money spent on a virtual collaboration workshop with a group of companies
Type 1 (DIRECT) OUTPUTS	Number of companies attending the workshop
Type 2 DRIVERS (LEADING INDICATORS)	Number of companies interested in participation in virtual collaborative projects
Type 3 COMPANY IMPACTS	Annual increased business trade by participating companies
Type 4 MACRO IMPACTS	Total increased business in a community, sector or cluster

Figure 2.3 – Measurement Categories

In the context of Benefits Realisation, we should be concentrating on Type 3 and Type 4 Measures.

If we are trying to track project progress (see Chapter 5 on Monitoring, Measuring and Correcting), we should be concentrating on Types 0, 1 and 2.

A similar and equally useful, easy to remember measurement classification scheme is ABCDE:

- Activities
- Behaviours
- Consequences
- Drivers
- Effects

2.4 Types of Measure

In measuring benefits, it is generally accepted that you should try to calculate a financial value. This can be challenging and in some cases may even be quite meaningless.

To see what might be possible in our project, it can be helpful to be aware of other important characteristics of measures:

Soft v Hard Measures

A soft measure is essentially an opinion or a judgement. You know you have a soft measure if two independent but equally competent observers reach a different conclusion.

Qualitative v Quantitative Measures

A Quantitative measure can be expressed as a number whereas a qualitative measure must be expressed as a statement. It is useful to separate Soft v Hard and Qualitative v Quantitative, as you can have a Soft Measure which is expressed Quantitatively e.g., 95% Customer Satisfaction.

Financial v Non-Financial Measures

This is easy – financial measures have an implied trading currency, non-financial do not. Again, you can have a quantitative non-financial measure e.g., 95% Team Morale.

Actual v Estimate

Sometimes it is not possible or economical to have a precise actual measure of a value. In this case you may work with an estimate, ideally with a stated margin of error.

Direct v Proxy

A Proxy measure infers the value of one measure from the measurement of another. For example, consumer confidence inferred from retail sales trends.

Aggregation v Deep Dive

Some measures are aggregations and averages that can conceal important information. One is reminded of the old saying "My head is in the oven and my feet are in the fridge but on average - I am fine".

Think of walking in your best shoes on a beach where the average depth of water is 3 inches but there could be places where it is 12 inches deep - or more!

Anecdotal v Actual

There is a myth that all benefits' numbers need to be Quantitative Actuals.

It is possible to achieve or manipulate a great set of numbers, for example customer feedback, which may conceal very significant issues that customers are encountering and are being ignored.

Depending on the nature of your project, anecdotes such as quotes and feedback may be a vital aspect of your benefits realisation tracking.

2.5 Benefits Realisation Example

For a simple example of Cost Benefit Analysis, you can check out the "Leadership Development Benefits Estimator Tool" on the (www.bioteams.com) blog.

A simple six-step process can be used for conducting a cost-benefits analysis on a proposed leadership development programme within an organisation:

1. Identify Leader's Potential Financial Impact
2. Assess Key Leader Skill Levels, Targets and Weightings
3. Estimate Financial Benefits of Leadership Development Intervention
4. Aggregate the Benefits to the whole target leader community
5. Consider the phasing of the benefits
6. Do the cost-benefits analysis

This approach considers the tricky issue of phasing the benefits over the project life. For example, you may conclude that only 50% of the benefits might accrue in the first year followed by 80% in year 2 and 100% in year 3.

Example Business Simulation

The PLAY-IT Business Simulation (described in 14.1) allows participants to engage with different types of project adoption and benefits realisation measures as they track the different projects they are managing and rolling out.

3. Sponsor Communications

Primary Focus
Leadership Communities

Key Objectives
Keeping the sponsor / steering group up-to-date on project status.

Key Chapter Topics

- Best Practices in running Stakeholder Meetings
- Asking for help effectively
- Communicating with Senior People
- Negotiating Skills
- Example Team Simulation

One of the key jobs for the project manager is keeping the project stakeholders up-to-date on project progress in both formal/steering meetings and less formal, small or 1-1 meetings. The other key job, often forgotten about, is to be able to ask for their help.

3.1 Best Practices for Stakeholder Meetings

Here are five key tips for making your stakeholder meetings more effective. The focus is mostly on the formal side but the principles also apply for the less formal, small or 1-1 meetings.

1. Sterile Cockpit - Maintain Focus!

Sterile Cockpit is an aviation term which means that during critical phases of the flight, such as take-off and landing, nothing else should be discussed by the flight crew apart from those two things. *Even if it is important, the crew must keep it for later.*

In operational meetings, this means stick to the agenda. No matter how interesting a new topic suddenly appears, don't get distracted if it is not directly pertinent to the main reason you are having the meeting.

The *FAA Sterile Cockpit* rule goes on to say that the cockpit team should avoid "activities such as eating meals, engaging in non-essential conversations within the cockpit, non-essential communications between the cabin and cockpit crews and reading publications not related to the proper conduct of the flight or not required for the safe operation of the aircraft." So, reading your email during an important meeting violates Sterile Cockpit.

2. Jackanory - No Story-telling i.e., reasons, explanations, justifications and causes.

Jackanory is rhyming slang in the Cockney tradition for 'Telling a Story.' When we tell a story about why something has occurred, we usually, without realising it, begin to defend and justify. This wastes time and energy. Instead of telling a story, we should practice only giving the absolute minimum facts to allow the meeting to determine the correct action. The time for stories is after the meeting - in the bar!

3. Sherlock Holmes - Reveal rather than conceal!

Sherlock Holmes was a famous but fictitious detective, who had a fantastic ability to uncover the truth in difficult circumstances. You should not expect your stakeholders to have the same level of investigative and deductive skills as Sherlock. You must make it easy for the leader of the meeting to get the information they need. So put it right out there without needing to be interrogated!

"Once you eliminate the impossible, whatever remains, no matter how improbable, must be the truth." Arthur Conan Doyle, creator of Sherlock Holmes, 1859-1930

4. Only Four Task States - Done, On Plan, At Risk and Missed

Ultimately, there are only four states a particular task or activity may be in. The sooner you can allocate the state to the task, the sooner you can decide what actions, if any, need to be taken.

Done or On Plan
Stakeholders can say "well done" - no further discussion is necessary in the meeting. Of course, they can challenge this statement or request more evidence!

At Risk or Missed
A new commitment is needed; help may be required from the stakeholders. They need to be happy that the new commitment is one that they can rely on given the previous one did not deliver.

We discuss Task States further in 5.4 and 5.6.

5. Five Key Meeting Roles - Customer, Facilitator, Timekeeper, Scribe and Sensor

Meetings tend to be much more successful if the following roles (or equivalent) are allocated to participants before the meeting starts.

Normally the main team "Customer" and facilitator will allocate these roles in advance:

Customer

The person who, given their role, has the strongest need for the meeting to produce a successful outcome. Being the customer, they decide if they are satisfied with the meeting. This is usually the main stakeholder/project sponsor but not always.

Facilitator

Steers and oils the running of the meeting and makes sure it follows the tips described above. Also makes sure the customer gets what they need (sometimes in spite of the customer!)

Timekeeper

Ensures that the meeting always knows where it stands with respect to time so that the appropriate amount can be allocated/reallocated to items in a sensible way.

Scribe

Takes notes during the meeting and produces the actions list afterwards.

Sensor

The objective is having somebody 'sense' the temperature of the meeting and to spot unhelpful group moods. For example, resignation or complaint. This role is sometimes also played by the Facilitator.

3.2 Asking for help – effectively!

One of the most common mistakes a project manager can make when engaging stakeholders is to report progress but not ask for help. If your stakeholders are on-the-ball, they will know this and ask you the question "What do you need me to do?" but you cannot rely on this. You always need to be thinking - 'what is my "ask"?' - so that you can make it effectively when the opportunity arises.

Here are some examples of the kind of things you might need to ask a stakeholder for help with:

- Can we adjust the priorities for the next deadline?
- Could you have a word with another stakeholder to see if you can get them to be more visibly supportive?
- Could you have a word with a major user to see if they can be more flexible with some of their requirements?
- Could you talk with the Head of Finance to see if I can get some more budget for project overtime?

To make an effective "ask" requires two things.

Firstly, you must be prepared to ask people more senior than you to do things for you and in effect become accountable to you. This can take courage.

Secondly, you must be able to make an effective request. According to an old colleague, Charles Spinosa from VISION (www.vision.com), an expert in the science of seeking, making and managing commitments, for a request to be effective it must have clear "conditions of satisfaction", namely five things:

1. **WHAT** is it that I need doing?
2. **WHO** needs to do it?
3. **WHEN** do I need it done by?
4. **HOW** will I judge if it has been fulfilled to my satisfaction?
5. The **PROTOCOL** to be adopted if "the performer" discovers they are unable to fully meet the request to my conditions of satisfaction

In our experience, senior stakeholders are generally very comfortable at being held accountable by others and will appreciate and respect your boldness, clarity and directness when you are making your requests.

3.3 Communicating with Senior People

Nancy Duarte, an American speaker, writer and CEO, has published an excellent article in the Harvard Business Review entitled "How to Present to Senior Executives."

She offers five great tips:

1. Summarise up front
Assume there is a good chance that a key person may have to leave suddenly, so use the first five minutes to summarise your pitch and any "asks" you may have.

2. Set expectations
Tell the group that you will be doing a short summary first, before going into the detail. This makes it less likely you will be constantly interrupted.

3. Create summary slides
Create slides that you can use if you get pressed to "cut to the chase".

4. Give them what they asked for

Be clear on why you were invited to meet the group and address this first before you address whatever else you need.

5. Rehearse

Before you meet them, run things through with a colleague who has senior communications experience and insist on frank feedback.

3.4 Negotiating Skills

A key skill in project management is negotiation. You will need to negotiate with Stakeholders. You will also need to negotiate with Key Influencers, Senior Users, Project Team members and Project Partners. So this skill, which we will summarise in this section, applies to your dealings across all communities.

One of most successful approaches to negotiation is known as principle-based or principled negotiation, made popular by the book "Getting to Yes" by Roger Fisher and William Ury. "Getting to Yes" (GTY), is the definitive text on modern negotiation practices and we will base most of this section on it. However, GTY is not the whole story and does have its weaknesses and criticisms but they are not relevant to our purposes here.

Principled negotiation stands in stark contrast to the more traditional "combative negotiations" where the objective is to emerge as "the winner". The theory of principled negotiation is that both parties need to be winners or the deal will be sour, not sustainable and consequently poison or even destroy the relationship between the two parties.

Principled negotiation is based around four simple principles:

1. *Separating the people from the problem*
The negotiation will go better and will be more collaborative if you can take ego and emotions out of the conversation.

2. *Focusing on interests rather than positions*
The difference between a position and an interest is best illustrated by a short story. A husband and wife both want an orange but they only have one between them. If they negotiate by positions, they will split the orange in two.

However, if the couple negotiate by interests, they may discover that the woman wants the orange peel to make jam and the man wants to eat the orange fruit. They can then agree a "win-win".

Note: Negotiation by positions often end up in a compromise which suits neither party.

3. *Generate options for mutual gain*
If focusing on interests is all about listening to each other, then generating options for mutual gain builds on this. It encourages both parties to work together, collaborate and create "win-win" options.

It is very important that this step is undertaken in a mood of speculation and brainstorming. The objective is to create lots of potential alternatives for review rather than to quickly find the best one – that comes in the next step.

4. *Insist on using objective criteria*
If you have done the previous steps well, you will have a reasonable list of "candidate solutions." Now you need to review this list in a systematic way, against a pre-agreed

set of criteria, in order to find the best solution for <u>both</u> parties.

Some critics of principled negotiation suggest that those using this approach can be easily exploited by hard-nosed negotiators on the other side who pretend to say all the right things but are just looking out for their own interests.

A powerful tool within principled negotiation which can protect against "power negotiators" is the *BATNA* (Best Alternative to a Negotiated Agreement). A BATNA supports the principle that no deal is better than a bad deal and that you can always walk away.

People sometimes wrongly describe a BATNA as the "bottom-line" negotiating position, below which you will walk away from the deal, but it is in fact quite different. For example, say you are meeting with a prospective supplier of a service that you wish to purchase. The BATNA in this case could simply be you sharing, near the beginning of the meeting, that you have already identified another supplier who can meet your requirements and costs. Before you go back to them to close the deal, you wish to see what this new supplier can offer.

3.5 Evidence-based decision-making

A project manager's two most important questions are "Who says?" and "So What?"

"Fake news" existed inside our organizations long before it became such a hot topic in the media today. If you are managing any business, venture, department, project, change or team you will need to become expert in distinguishing from what is real and what is just unexamined bulls**t.

These questions are two important tools within the discipline known as "Evidence-Based" decision-making in contrast to the more popular discipline of "Gut-Feel" decision-making. Other important tools within evidence based decision-making are *Root Cause Analysis* (described in 2.2) and the *Ladder of Inference* (described in 12.5).

However fake project news detection is not as easy as it seems! This is because such news often arrives with its credibility enhanced through longevity, repetition and senior endorsement. Fake news items can quickly become "elephants in the room" which everyone has got used to squeezing past and nobody even sees (or smells) anymore - except you!

However there are two very simple questions you can use to see if something passes the smell test and has real substance or not - "Who says?" and "So What?"

"Who says?" is about finding the original source of the news.

If you cannot locate the primary source it is a pretty good sign the news may be suspect. Also when you do locate the source you may well find that it says something very different from how it has been spun!

So let's say you have found the source of the project news in question and it looks pretty reliable - this is only the first part of your due diligence process. You now need to ask the question "if this is true does it mean what they say it means".

"So What" asks the question - is the interpretation of this "fact" as meaning X reasonable and the best among many potential interpretations.

One note of caution! Fake news elephant hunters inside projects and organisations may well become hunted themselves as people play *shoot the messenger*. Don't expect popularity - at least in the short-term.

However armed with these two questions, "Who says?" and "So What?" **plus** the other tools of evidence-based decision-making, Root Cause Analysis and the Ladder of Inference, **plus** a little bit of courage you can save your project and organization a lot of money and a lot of pain.

Example Business Simulation

The FUSION Business Simulation (described in 14.2) allows participants to negotiate with other departments as they try to reach agreement on sharing limited resources.

Further Reading

For a more detailed exploration of negotiation see "A Systematic Guide to Collaboration and Competition within Organizations" by Ken Thompson, March 2017.

4. Stakeholder Engagement

Primary Focus
Leadership Communities

Key Objectives
Using Change Management techniques to influence the
key stakeholders in order to win their visible support for
the project (Project Champions).

Key Chapter Topics
- Stakeholder Mapping
- Principles of Effective Engagement
- Creating Project Champions
- Making appropriate interventions
- Organisational versus Social Influence
- Example Business Simulation

4.1 Stakeholder Mapping

Stakeholders are typically senior individuals in an
organisation who have an interest (or stake) in the project
and who can either help or hinder its success.

A very useful technique at the beginning of any project is
to perform a Stakeholder Analysis on the key players who
will be impacted by or have an impact on the outcome.

This involves constructing a simple 3x3 matrix showing
Influence (*Organisational or Social*) on one axis and the
stakeholder's Attitude to the change (*Supporter, Neutral
or Opponent*) on the other, as shown in Figure 4.1. We will
explore the difference between Organisational and Social
Influence later in this section.

A stakeholder map helps to identify who the priority stakeholders are at the start of a project.

There are two critical categories of stakeholder *Influential Supporters* (Top Right) and *Influential Opponents* (Top Left).

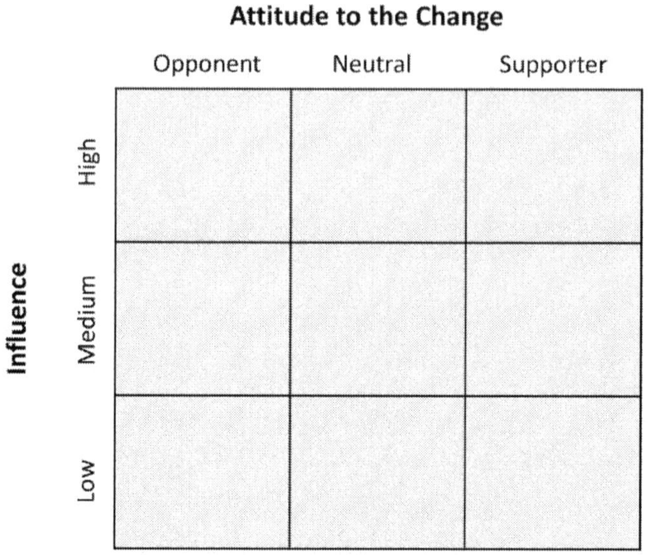

Attitude to the Change

Figure 4.1 – Simple Stakeholder Map

Best practice in engaging project stakeholders can be briefly summarised as:

1. Build your initial platform around influential supporters and potential supporters
2. Don't ignore influential opponents and potential opponents
3. These stakeholders will influence other stakeholders
4. Broaden your engagement platform as the project develops

4.2 Principles of Effective Engagement

There are four key aspects of effective individual engagement which are illustrated in Figure 4.2:

1. Insight and Relationship
2. Understanding and Influencing
3. Commitment
4. Support and Development

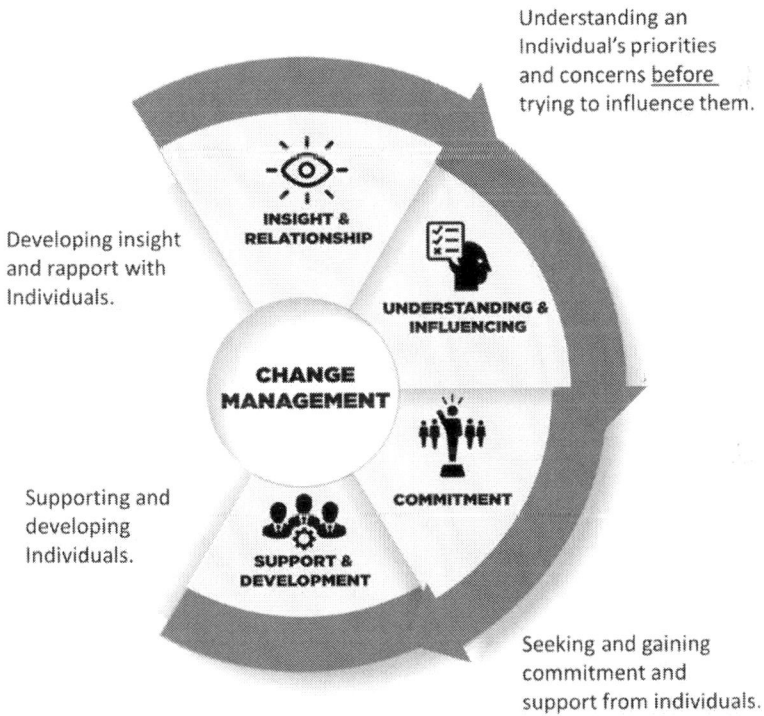

Figure 4.2 – Personal Engagement Model

These four aspects have an implied sequence 1 -> 2 -> 3 -> 4 to reflect three key change management principles, namely that you should:

- *Build rapport and relationships <u>before</u> you have serious conversations with people.*
- *Explore what people feel and want <u>before</u> you ask a person to commit to anything.*
- *Provide support to anyone who has made a commitment to you or is struggling.*

We can expand each of these further into more concrete interventions.

Insight & Relationships

Here you might consider:

- Gathering information about an individual.
- Meeting with an individual informally.

Understanding & Influencing

Here you might consider:

- Seeking an individual's views or advice about the proposed change.
- Working with an individual to help them deal with the change.
- Seeking feedback from an individual about issues they might have with you, with colleagues, or with the proposed change.

Commitment

Here you might consider:

- Engaging an individual about their views or advice on the proposed change.
- Asking an individual to support you and become a champion of the change.

Support & Development

Here you might consider:

- Helping and encouraging an individual to play a change champion role.
- Conducting a coaching and development conversation with an individual around change championing.

See also Appendix D: Key Principles of Change Management

4.3 Project Champions

One of the main objectives in engaging with a stakeholder is to see if they can become a 'Project (or Change) Champion'. There are three potential sub-roles involved in being a 'Project Champion':

- *Project Exemplars* are great examples of colleagues who have adopted the change wholeheartedly and effectively, appropriate to their organisational roles, so that you can point to these people as models of the change working well.

- *Project Advocates* listen to their colleagues and can persuasively argue the case for the change.
- *Project Ambassadors* promote the change in public and in group forums within the organisation.

When you ask a stakeholder to be a 'Project Champion', you are asking them to partner with you in <u>at least one</u> of these sub-roles. You will need to be clear which one (or more) you wish them to play, appropriate to their seniority and influence in the organisation.

For example, a junior colleague might be great as an operational project exemplar but not as good in front of a crowd as a project ambassador.

4.4 Making appropriate interventions

There is another very important question you must consider before you start making any interventions with your colleagues:

How do you know which intervention to make with each individual?

There are three things you need to determine beforehand:

Insight: How well do you know the individual and what is the health of your relationship?

Attitude: How do they view the proposed change?

Influence: How influential are they with their colleagues?

Let's look at each of these in a bit more detail:

Insight and Relationship
This is fairly obvious and relates directly to the engagement principles discussed earlier. If you lack insight or any form of relationship, you should address this before going any further. It is said that there is a bridge of rapport that exists between any two individuals. If the relationship is weak, then this bridge is like a fragile wooden structure but if it is strong, it is more like a robust concrete and steel construction. Only one of these bridges will allow 10-ton trucks to drive across it!

Attitude
You can place a person into one of three attitudes with respect to any potential future event - and upcoming change is no exception. Are they <u>for</u> it, are they <u>against</u> it or are they <u>neither</u> for nor against it!

In other words, are they *Supporters, Opponents* or *Neutrals*?

You need to make sure you don't confuse a relationship issue between an individual and yourself with their attitude to the change. It is possible for a colleague to have a poor relationship with you and be a supporter of the change proposal. Likewise, a colleague you get on with really well, could be an opponent!

Charles Spinosa has identified that there is, in fact, a fourth important attitude which is not normally captured in a standard change management Stakeholder Map – 'Ambivalence'. Ambivalence, without closer examination, may appear as either Neutrality or Opposition but this shallow interpretation can be very misleading.

Individuals can be ambivalent due to suspicion, confusion or lack of information, and if this is the case, once the individual's issue has been resolved, they may quickly spring to their authentic attitude which could be Support, Neutrality or Opposition.

This brings us to an important question:

How do you assess an individual's influence with their colleagues?

4.5 Organisational versus Social influence

These are the two main types of *Influence* in work situations.

Organisational influence depends on the person's position in either a hierarchy or a flat structure, their experience or length of service.

Social influence depends on the person's reputation and the extent of their social network within the organisation. Therefore, an individual with a strong reputation and a great social network could be very influential despite the fact that they might be quite junior and not the holder of one of the most senior job titles.

It is important to note that they need a good reputation and a good social network to have social influence. A person with just one of the two could be a *secret guru* (weak network) or a *friendly lightweight* (weak reputation).

This leads to another key question:

Q: Which is more powerful — organisational influence or social influence?

A: It depends!

Generally, in well-established or large companies, organisational influence counts for most, whereas in start-ups and small, non-traditional enterprises, social influence can be the most important.

Example Business Simulation

The COHORT Business Simulation (described in 14.3) allows participants to engage key stakeholders to secure their support for a major change programme.

Further Reading

For a more detailed exploration of Change Management and Influencing see "A Systematic Guide to Change Management" by Ken Thompson, July 2016.

5. Monitoring, Measuring and Correcting

<u>Primary Focus</u>
Target Communities

<u>Key Objectives</u>
Managing the execution of the tasks needed to deliver the project, tracking their effectiveness and making the necessary corrections.

<u>Key Chapter Topics</u>
- Task Monitoring
- Project Management Levers
- Project Contingency
- Project Review Meetings
- Project Rework
- Task Success Indicators
- Recap: Monitoring Fundamentals
- Example Business Simulation

5.1 Task Monitoring

It will have taken quite a bit of effort to get plans and schedules into a position where everyone is ready to commit to them and work can start. Before you give the green light, make sure you baseline the plan, or at least keep a copy, to reflect the starting position. It will give a reference point for comparison at key milestones throughout the project, as to what can be done better next time round.

It is also recommended that each member of the team has their own personal copy of the schedule so they can see how the overall project will be completed and not just their piece of the action. It will set the context and give everybody the chance to suggest any improvements.

Having done all of this, you are now ready to start.

The most important thing to acknowledge is that the very second someone starts work on their activities, the schedule is out of date. Do not do what many do and leave it too long before any monitoring is done, so it becomes almost impossible to take any meaningful remedial action.

Also, unlike some will have you believe, you cannot smell if a project is on track just through experience. It's not a great place to be when one of the key stakeholders asks you to demonstrate progress. There is no shortcut to a successful outcome.

It often comes as a surprise when it is realised that the main objective of monitoring is NOT just to keep the plan up to date or to report slippage – it's to take whatever action is necessary to keep the project on track and regain everyone's commitment to the latest version.

The best way of doing this is to get together as a team, review the status of each task and agree any corrective action. It is totally acceptable that new tasks are added, others removed and future estimates re-worked based on the knowledge gained so far. If this doesn't happen, then either something is wrong or you can predict the future!

5.2 Project Management Levers

If your project is running late or not meeting requirements or consuming too much resource or too much money, then what options do you have as a Project Manager? There are five potential levers you can adjust to get things back on track (Figure 5.1):

1.   Strategy
2.   Scope
3.   Quality
4.   Resource
5.   Time

Please note that some authors suggest there are just three levers – Scope, Resource and Time – however leaving out Strategy and Quality unnecessarily reduces the options at a project manager's disposal. In our opinion the more options the better!

Figure 5.1 – Project Management Levers

Let's look briefly at each of them, bearing in mind you may well have to apply more than one.

The first three levers, Strategy, Scope and Quality, address the Why, What and How questions of the project whereas the fourth and fifth levers, Resource and Time, address the Who and When aspects.

We have deliberately listed them in this sequence because if you haven't got the Why, What and How right then doing it faster is unlikely to produce a successful project outcome with your key communities.

The Strategy Lever addresses two fundamental questions – are the target outcomes still valid and, if so, are we going the right way about achieving them? There is an old Turkish proverb – "It's never too late to stop going down the wrong path". Valid outcomes from this lever are stopping the project, changing the project goals and altering the project approach.

For example:

- The project is stopped as it can no longer meet its Return on Investment targets
- The project can continue but its goal has changed to delivery of a defensive product as opposed to one of market leadership
- The original outsourcing approach is not working, and all work will now be performed in-house

The Scope Lever addresses two key questions – can we reduce what needs to be done and still achieve most of our goals and can we deliver some aspects of the project at a later stage? The authors remember a major internal IT project where we were told by external experts that based on the size of the outline data model, we had not one project but two. Unfortunately, that was not the message anyone wanted to hear so we carried on regardless and 18 months later, the external experts were proven to be 100% correct.

The Quality Lever addresses the question – are the quality processes built into the plan providing the requisite level of quality for the project goal? Requisite is an important word meaning "just right – not too high and not too low". The big bad wolf considered Goldilocks' porridge to be "requisite" in terms of temperature and taste.

Another example is in the use of review processes to be used for all the inputs and outputs from the project. A formal structured inspection process may be appropriate for high risk, high criticality deliverables but not for everything as one organisation discovered to its cost. The result was a significant slippage on all projects with no visible improvement in quality and a de-motivated workforce. In other words, a good process fell into disrepute due to its inappropriate use.

The Resource Lever addresses three questions:

- Have we got the requisite level of resourcing?
- Have our resources got the requisite skills and experience?
- Are they being organized in the optimum way?

In terms of the first question, we need to bear in mind the assertion in Fred Brooks' Law from his 1975 book 'The Mythical Man Month' i.e., – adding resource to a late project only makes it later, which applies in most cases but not universally.

It is worth reading Brook's book – however the bottom-line is this - while the new resources are 'getting on-board', they will distract the existing team who will need to spend considerable unplanned time bringing them up to speed.

With regard to the second question, are we clear who is learning on the job and who is doing work they might find boring, repetitive or demotivating?

In terms of the last question, we might for example decide to break big teams into smaller ones or the other way around to improve productivity. One way of looking at team size is the "Two Pizza Rule" popularised by Jeff Bezos at Amazon.com – i.e., if it takes more than 2 large pizzas to feed them then it is probably too big. A word of warning though – don't reduce the team size and increase the number of dependencies and hand-offs. This will have drastic repercussions.

The Time Lever addresses the question - can we deliver the project to the deadline based on what we now know? Like the Resource Lever, the Time Lever always needs to be addressed each time any of the first three levers are applied.

An important consideration here, the "do nothing" option, is to weigh up the impact of a potential slippage and consider whether it is better just to accept it. The authors remember the maxim "Accept no small slippage" which certainly used to be a key element of good project management mentoring.

It is always better to have one big slippage rather than six small ones - nothing erodes your trust and reputation like constant rolling slippage. Remember, when you negotiate your new project end date, it is always good to ask yourself and your team – will I be back for more next month? This is, sadly, a common attribute of large projects where the success stories are few and far between. It's always best to break the project down into delivery phases based on business value and get something out there. In today's competitive market, velocity is often the prime driver, but each project needs to be uniquely approached and planned with all five levers in mind.

5.3 Project Contingency

'If you know you need it, then it's not contingency.'

One of the project manager's many roles is to update and re-issue the schedule, having added the actual effort, revised the forecasts to complete and made every effort to contain any slippage that could compromise the overall end date.

To increase the chances of success and for good practice, it is advisable to have a limited amount of contingency in each phase or iteration of the project. It is not to be used for anything other than adjusting estimates and certainly not to increase the scope and sneak in any late changes.

If the project has a governance board or steering committee, it may be worth asking them to approve all uses of contingency as this will give them an understanding of why it is necessary and to ensure that it is being used properly.

At the appropriate milestone, any unused contingency can be either removed to reduce the overall effort and cost or carried over to the next phase, bearing in mind the amount of contingency should reduce as the project progresses and the unknowns, risks and issues are resolved.

5.4 Project Review Meetings

The frequency of the monitoring meetings will depend on several factors:

- The duration of the project or iteration
- What works best for the team
- The criticality of the project
- The needs of the stakeholders

Many prefer a 15-minute session every morning before any work starts where the previous day's work is reviewed as well as what needs to happen today and where any help is needed to progress a task. Others prefer a more formal weekly meeting but that's about it. Any longer period between meetings will make it meaningless as projects have a habit of introducing the unexpected and a lot can happen on a project in a week!

A widely used methodology within the agile community is Scrum. It recommends the daily 15-minute stand-up mentioned above. Work is broken down into a series of iterations, known as Sprints, of no longer than two weeks duration. At the end of the sprint, there should be something to demonstrate to stakeholders. There should also be a review of each sprint as it completes, known as a retrospective, that looks at the performance of the team – what went well / not so well.

For further reading, we recommend a book by the co-creator Jeff Sutherland: SCRUM: The Art of Doing Twice the Work in Half the Time.

Whatever process or method you use, the critical outcome is to always ensure that all impacted parties are fully up to speed on project status and there are no known surprises lurking in the detail. An excellent way of reporting progress is to visualize it on a progress board, ideally displayed in the project area. Everyone can then see the latest position as each task is either outstanding, in progress, or completed. It is much easier to see where any bottlenecks and delays are inhibiting progress by using coloured 'stickies' in each of the three categories (outstanding, in progress, or completed); the team can then work together to remedy the situation and move forward.

See also 3.1 and 11.2 for more on good meeting practices.

5.5 Project Rework

There is one other question that needs to be answered before too much effort is spent:

How is Rework going to be managed from a monitoring perspective?

Rework is inevitable once the users get their hands on whatever deliverables have been produced for their review. It's not possible to correctly interpret all of their wants and needs, in whatever format they may take; often they won't know themselves until they can see it.

Whatever you decide, Rework needs to be transparent and tracked separately. An additional activity on the plan at phase level is a good idea. It will also provide the data needed for learning in the next phase and also future projects. Try not to introduce a bureaucratic change process that has no benefit other than providing protection for the team. This will cause conflict as the objective is to collectively deliver something of real value to the entire organisation.

5.6 Task Success Indicators

Tasks are either 0% complete or 100% complete; there is no middle ground. Planning tools can only calculate how much you are through the time and money; they cannot calculate how far you are through the business value being delivered. If asked on the progress of a task and the answer is 30% complete – what can the recipient do with that information?

This raises the issue of how to track value and a very useful technique is "Earned Value Project Tracking". The authors learned this the hard way. We worked on a project which had a budget of £1.2M and was scheduled to deliver in 12 months. For the first 10 months, the project manager reported £100K of work done each month – so in their estimation based on budget and resource spend after month 10, the project was over 80% done (£1M/£1.2M).

Then in month 11, the project manager started to track the work remaining rather than the work completed and concluded that there was 50% of the project still to do. This meant that the project team had to run for another year but with no more budget made available from the customer.

Effective estimating of work to complete would obviously have helped here. Even better would have been "Earned Value" where, before you start, you allocate a number of units of business value to key deliverables. These are then tracked with the important caveat that you don't count any units as a % complete until the appropriate deliverable is fully completed.

A task can only be marked as 100% completed when all of its exit criteria have been met; often referred to as the Definition of Done. What these criteria are, should be documented in the plan e.g. design agreed – proceed to build or documentation agreed and signed off by all parties or demo to customer complete and signed-off. There should then be no opportunity for any further work to be done on the task. If it is impacted by a later change, then add a new task to the schedule – don't reactivate the old one. See also 3.1 for more information on task states.

5.7 Recap: Monitoring Fundamentals

This chapter can be summed up in terms of your response to three key questions:

Question 1: Are you managing or presiding?

Earlier in this chapter we introduced the five Project Management levers:

1. Strategy
2. Scope
3. Quality
4. Resource
5. Time

It is important to be aware that if you, as the Project Manager, do not have authority to change at least one of these levers then you are not able to manage the project. In this scenario you are not managing anything, merely presiding as a figurehead and you are the prime candidate for becoming the scapegoat when it goes wrong. Never forget that when a date goes public, it's your date – no-one else's, so do whatever is required to maintain it.

Question 2: Are you correcting or keeping score?

We mentioned earlier that the whole point of project tracking is to enable you to spot where you need to make corrections before it is too late. Likewise, if you are managing project risks, it is easy to let the risk register become a depository of risks which are about to happen. The only purpose of tracking risks is to identify when something is likely to go wrong so that you have time to mitigate against it.

Question 3: What do you want to be remembered for?

Remember the project management maxim "Accept no small slippage?" Another one is that "Project users have short memories." Even though your users are up in arms about the project taking longer than planned or costing more, believe it or not, they will forgive and forget this after the project goes live. However, they will not forgive and forget poor quality or lack of utility or lack of fitness for purpose because every single time they use the outputs from the project, they will be reminded of how bad it is and how culpable you are!

Example Business Simulation

The CREW Work and Team Management Business Simulation (described in 14.4) allows participants to allocate, track and manage project tasks for their team.

6. Commitment Management

<u>Primary Focus</u>
Primarily Target Communities but also Leadership and Project Team Communities.

<u>Key Objectives</u>
To ensure there is a solid approach for managing accountability on the project, i.e., the making, tracking and adjusting of commitments and promises.

<u>Key Chapter Topics</u>
- The three types of process in any project
- Promise, Responsibilities and Guarantees
- Commitment-based Management
- Example Business Simulation

6.1 Material, Information & Commitments

There are just three main types of process inside projects – the first two are very visible and explicit but the last one is often invisible and implicit, which is where the problems begin!

<u>Materials Processes</u> transport or transform physical material from one place or state to another. For example, raw materials turn into work-in-progress which then turn into end products; or end products which are shipped from a warehouse to a customer's premises.

<u>Information Processes</u> transmit or transform information from one place or state to another. For example, customer orders turn into customer delivery notes, which over time should turn into invoices, which should then turn into

remittance advices; or a financial payment is transmitted from the customer's bank account to your company's bank account.

These two types of process are very visible and can be clearly mapped out on flowcharts so there is no ambiguity. However, neither of these processes would happen at all if a third category did not exist – <u>Commitment Processes</u>!

If an individual working for a customer did not ask another individual working for your company for a service or product (by voice, email or letter), there would be no orders and no product would ever be shipped. If the individual at your company did not agree payment terms with the customer individual then no money would ever be transferred to your company's bank account.

These transactions are examples of Commitment Processes which are often just referred to as Commitments, Agreements and Promises.

Commitment Processes are generally described in much less rigorous ways than Materials or Information Processes. This leads to all kinds of misunderstandings and communication breakdowns in projects, teams and organisations.

To address this problem, it requires a discipline known as *Commitment Management* which we will introduce here. However, we first need to explore the meaning of some everyday language and terms which can often trip us up.

6.2 Promises, Responsibilities and Guarantees

To best appreciate how to achieve team member accountability, we first need to appreciate the difference between a *promise, a responsibility* and a *guarantee.*

During the UK floods, which were widely reported on the TV news a few years ago, we heard a lot about defences failing and phrases being bandied about by engineers and managers such as "a once in a hundred years" event and "could never have been envisaged." However, when you hear these types of explanations, it is always interesting to listen out for the commitment <u>or lack of it</u> in the speaker's voice.

Often organisations, in the worthy name of professionalism, quality and standards, freely hand out **responsibilities** but neglect the more valuable **commitments**.

What's the difference between a Promise and a Responsibility?

For example, in the floods scenario, a responsibility is to make sure that all maintenance is fully up to date on a flood barrier. Usually, there is no shortage of people with statements such as these in their job descriptions. However, this is a million miles short of somebody making a *promise* that the barrier will not fail!

Do people in your target community, project team or stakeholder groups hold real commitments (aka promises) or are they just responsibilities? If they don't hold promises then the project will fail and it will be nobody's fault (with the likely exception of you - the project manager!)

Does anyone in your team get held to account if the project's "flood defences" fail?

It's not about "the blame game" but rather the vital missing ingredient in many projects' organisational governance and oversight systems!

Promises have to be held voluntarily and willingly; they cannot be ordered or demanded. So, if someone is asked to hold a promise, for example, that the flood defence will not fail, then it is perfectly reasonable for them to say that they need to discuss and negotiate the "supports" which would need to be in place for them to be able to make such a promise with confidence.

This is a valuable conversation in any project, team or organisation - what would need to happen or change for you to be able to commit to a promise which is valuable but currently seems out of reach?

If this conversation is conducted well, it will identify changes that nobody has really thought about and even uncover major flaws in existing designs. This is because we automatically think in a totally different way about things when we feel truly accountable for the outcomes. Anticipated promises give their potential promise-holders a powerful kind of instinctive x-ray vision of what is really missing!

Guarantees
Quite often people resist promises because they believe they are being asked to give guarantees. A promise is no more a guarantee than a responsibility is a promise!

A pilot promises to fly the passengers safely to their destination on time and will die attempting to honour this promise, but sadly they cannot guarantee that there will always be a satisfactory outcome - every single time.

However, the reality is that no matter how professional your people are and how complete their responsibilities are, unless you have gone beyond this and secured their promises, you will regularly fail to live up to your implied and explicit customer commitments.

6.3 Commitment-based Management

In their excellent article from the Harvard Business Review (April 2007) "Promise-Based Management: The Essence of Execution" by Donald Sull and Charles Spinosa, the authors suggest that the parties to any promise should first go through three phases of conversation together if it is to be a real promise which can be counted upon:

1. *Achieving a meeting of minds* - where the requestor and the provider explore key questions such as: What do you mean? Do you understand what I mean? What should I do? What will you do? Who else should we talk to?

2. *Making it happen* - where the provider executes on the promise but keeps the requestor totally in the loop on how it is going and if the standards of performance need to be renegotiated for any reason.

3. *Closing the loop* - where the requestor agrees that the provider has delivered what was asked for or failed to do so. This affords both parties with the opportunity to offer each other feedback on how they could work more effectively in the future and improving the quality of other promises they might make together.

On a project, there will be a multitude of potential promises (in fact - a "network of promises").

For example:

- Promises held by the project manager to external stakeholders and vice versa
- Promises held by team members to one or more project managers
- Promises held by supporting project managers to the lead project manager
- Promises held by project managers to team members (typically around support and development)
- Promises held by team members to each other (typically around helping each other)

If any one of these classes of promise is missing, it is unlikely that the project will achieve its goals.

6.4 Making and managing promises

Fred Kofman, in a chapter entitled "Impeccable Coordination" from his excellent book "Conscious Business", offers some tips on how to spot "weasel" commitments, purely by the language used.

For example:

- Somebody needs to do something (when everybody is responsible then nobody is responsible).
- Sharon will do that (only an individual can make a commitment - nobody can commit on behalf of anyone else).

- I assume that's OK with you (people have to be asked if they commit – it cannot be assumed).
- Let me see what I can do (this is no commitment whatsoever).
- I will do my best (this is only slightly better).

One practical rule that you can use when evaluating whether you are happy with a promise being offered is this:

'Would you accept such a promise from your airline pilot as you go on holiday with your family?'

Now re-read the last two statements in light of this rule!

Kofman points out that there are only six clear answers we can give when a commitment is sought from us:

1. Yes, I promise
2. No, I don't commit
3. I need clarification before I can answer
4. I promise to give you an answer by this date ("commit to commit")
5. I can promise to get it done if, for example, you help me for two hours or do this bit of it
6. I counter offer - I can't do x but I could do y

In terms of making promises, Kofman suggests we need to have four standards to maintain our integrity at the very moment we commit:

- Do I understand the request?
- Do I believe I have the necessary tools and resources to fulfil the request?
- Do I believe the other people I depend on will deliver? (As the buck stops with me to deliver – I cannot blame them.)

- Have I anticipated and considered the foreseeable risks? (Note the foreseeable risks – I cannot predict the future.)

Finally, in the real world, we frequently break our promises - we need to be able to deal with this properly when it happens otherwise there will be a spiral of distrust and resentment between the impacted parties.

Kofman suggests these four practical steps for making an apology regarding a broken promise:

1. The moment the promise becomes a risk, we should call the person who made the request so they can take precautions. The golden rule is - we should always put ourselves in their shoes.
2. We should offer an explanation and an apology that we are breaking our promise. However, make sure it does not sound like a justification story - just the facts!
3. We should ask the person how this is a problem for them. Then we should listen carefully and renegotiate a new promise to take care of this.
4. Finally, we should reflect and learn from the breakdown in our promise for the next time.

To dig deeper into the discipline of *Commitment-Based Management,* we recommend you check out Professor Donald Sull's 3-part short video series on *YouTube* entitled: "Promise based management: London Business School"

Example Business Simulation

The CREW Work and Team Management Business Simulation (described in 14.4) allows participants to engage with their project team members around their project commitments.

7.   Word of Mouth

<u>Primary Focus</u>
Target Communities

<u>Key Objectives</u>
Creating a positive view of the project with those who can help accelerate its adoption within their community.

<u>Key Chapter Topics</u>
- From Stakeholder to Community Engagement
- The difference between a community and a crowd
- Super-connectors and word of mouth
- Engaging Community Influencers
- Example Business Simulation

7.1 From Stakeholder to Community Engagement

In Chapter 4 - Stakeholder Engagement - we explored ways to influence senior stakeholders, colleagues or team members. This is a critically important aspect of project management but often this is only the first part of what is necessary for project success.

You will need to go beyond senior leaders and extend into the bigger target communities who are the primary audience for your project. In moving from small group engagement to large-scale community engagement, many new challenges will be encountered such as:

- Engaging with people, some of who, at best, we barely know

- The impracticality of face-to-face and one-on-one engagement due to scale
- The reliance on virtual and one to many interactions
- The importance of key influencers in the target communities who can help or hinder the project

To be successful in large-scale target community engagement, we also need to understand some important points:

- The difference between a community and a crowd - and why it matters
- The role of super-connectors and word of mouth
- Key types of activities you need in your change campaign

7.2 The difference between a community and a crowd

So, what is the difference?

You might say that a community has a shared interest or purpose, but a crowd does not. However, a crowd of football supporters have a shared interest and yet they are still a crowd. So shared interest is necessary but not sufficient to being a community.

You might then go on to say that a community is of a scale which permits regular interaction between most of its members, but a crowd does not. There is something in that, but it is also possible to be part of a very small crowd which is even smaller than some communities. So frequent member interaction is also necessary but not sufficient to being a community.

A good way to appreciate the difference between a community and a small crowd is to think of the difference between a Sports Team and a Fitness Club.

People attend a fitness club to use the exercise equipment and incidentally meet other members. The primary glue is the shared access to expensive equipment and facilities. Meeting other users is not an essential part of the experience. However, people join a Sports Team to play team sports and meeting other players is an essential part of that experience.

The thing which makes a community different from a crowd, in our opinion, is that in a community there is a deep network of relationships spanning the whole community whereas in a crowd there are lots of little localised clusters of relationships. Whilst there may be links between the different clusters in a crowd, there is nothing like the extent of cross-network relationships which there are in a community.

Another way to understand the difference is to say that a community is a "Peer Network" but a crowd is a "Star Network". In a community there is a horizontal network of relationships between peers whereas in a crowd there are small numbers of "stars" and each member relates to these stars (vertically) much more than they relate to each other (their peers).

Why does this matter for large-scale community engagement?

The main thing is that it is much easier to engage a community than a crowd. This is because a crowd is really a collection of discrete small groups (clusters) and if you communicate with one of these clusters, there is no guarantee that they will pass on your communications to anyone else because they may only be loosely connected to these other clusters. However, in a community, the wide network of relationships makes it much easier to propagate any message.

Does this mean you cannot bring change to a crowd? No, of course not. It just means it will be more difficult and you will need to work harder. You really need to think of a crowd as segmented into many mini-communities which are only very loosely linked. To engage such a crowd, you need to engage with each of these mini-communities separately which adds up to much more effort than if it was just one community.

7.3 Super-connectors and word of mouth

A key aspect of engaging effectively with a community is to try and identify the key people in the network who have a) the most relationships and b) the best authority then having done this, try to collaborate with them to pass on your messages. Let's call them "super-connectors" but they can also be referred to as community leaders, key influencers and opinion leaders.

There are two types of authority – organisational authority (positional) and social authority (reputational). We will focus our discussion here on reputational, however the approach can be adapted to communities where organisational authority dominates.

It is important to remember that super-connectors should have both a good network and a good reputation. If they have a good network and a poor reputation they will just be annoying noise generators within the community. On the other hand, if they have a great reputation (perhaps for their expertise in some topic) but are badly connected, they may be of little use.

However, one important caveat applies. If your change message is opposed or discredited by an expert with a small network, it is quite likely that their opinion will get picked up and transmitted by other community members with much bigger networks and your change initiative may then suffer from a credibility issue.

Albert-László Barabási, a former Professor at the University of Notre Dame, has researched extensively into the concept of what he calls "scale-free networks" in natural, technological and social systems, from the cellular telephone to the World Wide Web and online communities.

Barabasi has written an excellent book on the subject – "Linked: The New Science of Networks" in which he defines a "scale-free network" as a network whose degree distribution follows a power law. In layman's terms, what this means is that a small percentage of the nodes in such networks have significantly higher connectivity than the other nodes. Barabasi explains how the scale-free network structure applies to human networks which have "super-connectors" i.e., those who have much higher levels of connectivity than anyone else in the network.

A key element of promoting change in a community is identifying and collaborating with these super-connectors in order to spread the change throughout the community. It is interesting to note that you can also have super-connectors within a crowd but to a much lesser degree.

Working with super-connectors is a double-edged sword. They can be difficult, arrogant and impetuous. They can oppose you. They can turn from supporters into opponents overnight. They can make your life very difficult. They can have a huge sense of their own importance. They may be hugely demanding of your time and attention. They can delay you with suggested changes to your approach.

However, super-connectors are a fact of community change but without them, your change will fail. Super-connectors can create a "word of mouth" dynamic within the community where everyone is talking about your change. It is entirely up to you to establish whether they are saying good things or bad things about it!

7.4 Engaging Community Influencers

Most target communities have key individuals who are very influential. They can use this influence for or against your project. They can also choose to ignore your project which could also make it more difficult for you.

The first stage is to identify these people within the community. It may be that some of them are very visible and obvious and by engaging with them carefully, you may also build up a profile of the characteristics and meeting places of the others.

Normally, the next stage is to try and get these influencers into an early co-invention conversation about the change in order to seek their support. You want to see if they are positive and will help you. Alternatively, if they are lukewarm, neutral or opposing, you need to listen to their advice and find a way to re-engage them later.

The techniques are the same as those we have already described in Chapter 4 – Stakeholder Engagement namely:

- Insight and Relationship
- Understanding and Influencing
- Commitment
- Support and Development

The important proviso is that there could be a lot more of them to engage with and you may not always be able to do so on a face-to-face or one to one basis. We will cover this type of virtual engagement in the next chapter (Chapter 8 - User Adoption).

Example Business Simulation

The SPREAD Business Simulation (described in 14.5) allows participants to identify super-connectors and exploit positive 'words of mouth' throughout their project rollout campaigns.

Further Reading

For a more detailed exploration of change management and engaging communities see "A Systematic Guide to Change Management" by Ken Thompson, July 2016.

8.   User Adoption

<u>Primary Focus</u>
Primarily Target Communities but also Leadership and Project Team Communities.

<u>Key Objectives</u>
Developing and executing strategies to move the user community up the adoption ladder, stage by stage.

<u>Key Chapter Topics</u>
- •   Four Types of Adoption Task
- •   User Adoption Models
- •   Risks of email in mass adoption
- •   Example Business Simulation

8.1 Four Types of Adoption Task

To effectively engage a community to adopt a project, you need to consider four main types of activity:

- • Preparedness Activity
- • Community Influencer Activity
- • Risk Mitigation Activity
- • User Adoption Activity

These four types of activity are not mutually exclusive. For example, a specific preparedness activity might also mitigate against an important adoption risk.

Preparedness Activity

This kind of activity is normally conducted before a campaign commences and its purpose is to lay important foundations which will make future engagement activities more effective. Typical examples include setting up steering groups or customer representative panels and developing appropriate written and multimedia assets to support the engagement.

Community Influencer Activity

We have already described Community Influencer Activity in Chapter 7 - Word of Mouth.

Risk Mitigation Activity

Strictly speaking, risk mitigation activities are special cases of preparedness or community influencer activities. However, they are so important and so frequently missing from project adoption campaigns that we will treat them here distinctly.

When you are planning your campaign, you need to include a risk analysis of what might go wrong. There are two risk perspectives – risks within your control and risks which are outside of your control. Failing to engage certain high-profile influencers would be an example of a risk within your control. Finding yourself in competition with a similar or competing rollout within the same community, might be an example of a risk outside of your control.

Both these risks are entirely foreseeable so specific avoidance and mitigation activities can be planned to:

a) Reduce the risk of them happening and/or

b) Allow you to respond effectively and quickly if they do occur.

There are other types of risk, such as your company being acquired or the government falling, which might be much more difficult to foresee. In this case, whilst it may not be possible to identify specific mitigations in advance, you can still structure your change project in a way that might make them less impactful. For example, by building in contingency for time, budget or resources which you do not plan to use if things go well.

A vital risk mitigation activity is to build the necessary early warning systems to alert you if a risk starts to materialise. Such systems are typically reporting mechanisms built around the leading indicators of success. You will have identified these as part of your plan for measuring project success through a Balanced Scorecard approach (See Chapter 2).

User Adoption Activity

This final type of activity may represent the bulk of your time and effort in a project adoption programme. These are the activities which directly move individuals in the community from one level of adoption to the next.

8.2 User Adoption Models

A useful tool in developing adoption activities is the AIDCA Engagement model which is similar to the change adoption model described earlier in Chapter 4 - Stakeholder Engagement. However, these are more suited to communities and summarised in Figure 8.1.

ATTENTION	Grabbing a person's attention for your idea
INTEREST	Gaining a person's interest in your idea based on relevance
DESIRE	Connecting your idea with a person's personal wants and needs
CONVICTION	Providing convincing evidence of your idea
ACTION	Gaining commitment to the action you want the people to take

Figure 8.1 – AIDCA Engagement Model

To be able to monitor your success, you will also need a "Community Adoption Model" plus some mechanism for identifying when individuals move forwards (or backwards) based on some observable behaviours which you can then build into reporting systems.

For example, the SPREAD Simulation (described at the end of this chapter and in more detail in 14.4), uses a five-point Adoption Model shown in Figure 8.2.

In addition, at any level (1-4) below "Sustaining" on the model, a potential user can REJECT (returning to level 0) the change altogether thus becoming closed to any further engagement on the topic.

A crucial element of user adoption activity is to create systems which allow you to track, not just the adoption, but the costs and, where possible, the benefits of any change campaign. The costs are usually easy to track as they are driven by the activities. The benefits are usually related to the adoption levels and can be harder to track and may also extend well beyond the life of the change campaign.

ADOPTION LEVEL	ADOPTION CHARACTERISTICS
SUSTAINING (5)	Embracing the change on an on-going basis and prepared to champion the change to others
USING (4)	Embracing the change on a trial basis but not yet a sustaining habit or practice
COMMITTED (3)	Committed to the change in principle but not yet embracing it
AWARE (2)	Aware of the proposed change but have not yet formed a solid opinion on it
UNAWARE (1)	Not aware of the proposed change

Figure 8.2 – Community Adoption Model

8.3 Risks of email in adoption

In large scale community engagement, it is inevitable that many of the user adoption activities will involve email and other forms of electronic communications. In addition, many of these will also be of a one-to-many nature rather than the more personal one-on-one communications.

These two facts create certain risks including:

- "Mailshot syndrome", where the messages attract a very low response (both open rates and action rates)
- Getting caught in SPAM filters
- Getting lost in the sheer volume of messaging traffic
- Negative reactions if your messages appear to be unsolicited
- Negative feedback loops, especially if using social media
- Tendency to over-estimate the levels of user engagement achieved

There are three specific principles you can apply to help you minimise these risks:

#1 Respect Data Protection and Personal Privacy

You need a person's express permission to email them – you cannot just email somebody whose details you found on a list. Data Protection legislation is becoming tighter year after year with huge fines in place for companies who flout the rules. Key areas to look out for include suppression list management, where it is your responsibility to maintain and manage accurate lists of both people who have agreed to be mailed on a topic and those who have asked not to be mailed. It is also becoming increasingly important that people actively opt-in to receiving your emails as opposed to the older system of them having to opt-out if they do not wish to be mailed. In addition, permission is granted only on a specific topic – i.e., just because you previously emailed someone about topic X does not allow you to email them about topic Y unless X and Y can be shown to be clearly linked.

#2 Normal social etiquette rules still apply digitally

Sometimes when we communicate via electronic messaging, we try to get to the point too quickly and in so doing we violate the normal rules of rapport building and social etiquette. It is nearly always better to take an extra email or message to build social rapport before we push for some form of commitment.

#3 Blend the digital and the personal

Research shows that purely digital engagement does not build anything like the levels of rapport you can build with face to face communication. Therefore, make sure that you have built as much physical interaction into your campaign as possible.

Examples include lunch-time briefings with small groups, large group presentations and presentation/attendance at relevant conferences targeted at a particular community.

Where you do not have the time or capacity for physical meetings, you can always build in telephone calls, which although not as good as face-to-face meetings, are still much more engaging than any form of email or messaging.

Example Business Simulation

The SPREAD Business Simulation (described in 14.5) allows participants to practice different types of user adoption activities within their project rollout campaign.

Further Reading

For a more detailed exploration of community adoption see "A Systematic Guide to Change Management" by Ken Thompson, July 2016.

9.   Planning & Scheduling

Primary Focus
Primarily Project Team Communities but also Leadership and Target / User Communities.

Key Objectives
To introduce the project environment, the basic disciplines of project planning and practical guidance for the real-world challenges.

Key Chapter Topics
- The challenging habitat of the Project Manager
- Project Planning 101
- Project Planning in the real world
- Tips BEFORE you make your plan
- Recap: Planning Fundamentals
- Example Business Simulation

9.1 The challenging habitat of the Project Manager

In an ideal world, there would be no need to plan or schedule anything.

The business landscape would comprise of self-managing, autonomous teams, whose members are encouraged to pick and choose their work from a pre-prioritised product backlog or equivalent, safe and secure in the knowledge that everyone is fully aware of what everyone else is doing.

This is a world without dependencies or constraints, either internal or external, and completed work can be delivered to customers at will. Nothing can get in the way; no bottlenecks or logjams.

Business and technical architectures would be loosely coupled and each piece of work would be small, easy to deploy and even easier to back out, in the unlikely event that something doesn't go to plan, even if one existed.

All work would flow smoothly, with the amount in progress totally under control and visible. Limits on what can be handled at any given time would be known and understood by all, with any constraints elevated and removed quickly, with minimal impact.

Workers would be happy and customers delighted, many of whom would emerge as the best of advocates, dramatically reducing the marketing budget. The bottom line would ooze profit; the competition would be blown away.

Are there any organisations that work like this?

Definitely!

Were there a lot of hard yards to be made before they got there?

Absolutely!

So why doesn't everyone strive to work this way?

Well that's for another book!

Most of us, whether we are part of a core team or project partners, have chosen to plan and schedule in a more traditional manner. Constraints abound, whether they be people, process or technology related, and it needs a transformational leader to confront these impostors and convince the powers that be that something needs to be done in order to compete. A seat at the decision-making table needs to be earned.

Two influential military strategists, born two millennia apart, took a pragmatic approach to planning:-

'A good plan today is better than a perfect plan tomorrow' – George S. Patton

'Plan for what is difficult while it is easy, do what is great while it is small' – Sun Tzu

There are similarities to today's project management world. We can all learn from these two leaders.

Project Managers work almost exclusively in an intense, pressurised environment and the only difference is that jobs and reputations are on the line and not lives – thankfully.

It seems apt, therefore, to start with a war story. It mirrors many of the larger programmes, both historical and in-flight, where a few scars will no doubt remain. The example comes from the world of technology but it could have happened anywhere.

Not so long ago, there was only one way to do things and that was sequential. In this world, one phase followed another once all the exit and entry criteria were met – commonly referred to in the technology world as waterfall development. The *Agile Manifesto* was still just a twinkle in the eyes of those who instinctively knew there was a better way of doing things.

In waterfall development, big was beautiful and the order of play was regimented. The larger the project, the more stars you had pinned to your collar. If a level of complexity was sprinkled into the mix, then so much the better.

'We need those service providers to earn their corn' was the customer battle-cry.

THE most important document was the project plan, closely followed by its supporting schedule. These were the two critical deliverables and ones that gave the grown-ups a feeling of security and a strange, somewhat misplaced level of satisfaction that all will be well. To paraphrase a former British Prime Minister – 'We have in our hands a piece of paper.'

The questions that need to be answered are: –

- What relevance do they have?
- How do they contribute to a successful outcome?
- Who are their customers?

This is not to say that all plans and schedules produced in the traditional way should be challenged or dismissed as not fit for purpose but many are tinged with a dubious level of optimism, often crafted to satisfy the wishes of the major stakeholders and sponsors.

'It will get them off our backs for a while' is a statement often overheard in many coffee bars. A culture of fear and blame was not uncommon.

However, if there could be an environment where innovation and creativity were encouraged and everybody works as a team, continuously improving their ways of working, all projects would have a greater chance of success – wouldn't they?

Surely no-one would come up with something like this as a blueprint?

A world where: -

- Business cases for projects are approved, almost without exception, well before the core team and /

or project partners are engaged or the return on investment comes under intense scrutiny.

- Projects are initiated and given the green light without due care and attention to any existing constraints or potential risks.
- Requirements are documented and signed-off in user blood before any detailed work can start.
- A strict change control process is then enforced, at a time when the stakeholders' wants and needs are at their most vague.
- Plans are produced which evidence the processes and methods that MUST be used giving the teams very limited opportunity for improvements.
- Schedules are produced which show a detailed work breakdown structure, with every single task identified all the way through to project completion. Contingency is frowned upon.
- Resources are allocated based on their availability and not always based on competency and / or an optimized flow of work.
- Estimates are not always given by the people doing the work and are often compromised to keep the end date within acceptable boundaries.
- Sponsors turn up to the scheduled governance or progress meetings to find out what's going on as opposed to resolving issues and re-prioritising as appropriate.
- The first time the users are given a working product or service to review is when it is at its most expensive to change. This may be months or even years after the original idea was formulated.

The list is endless. This is a war zone, make no mistake!

Although a number of these have little direct correlation to planning and scheduling per se, they do drive the way the work works. The chances of a successful outcome are remote but at least it explains why an unacceptably high percentage of large projects fail to deliver their promised benefits.

The real killer is the complete lack of any community spirit. This means there is only one place to point the finger when things go wrong - and that's straight at the project manager. Sadly, this suits some cultures and once again, it takes transformational leadership to turn things around. Many initiatives start from a bottom-up groundswell but this can only go so far without executive sponsorship.

Fix the culture and behaviours will change. Only then will plans and schedules become credible, jointly owned and supported by the entire community and not just the project manager. The focus then turns on its head to one of achieving organisational goals, possibly for the first time, and not just those of a particular team.

9.2 Project Planning 101

Before delving too deeply, it is worth recapping on the basic theory of how projects should be planned (see Figure 9.1). There are many different methods but most would agree they are all a variation on these 10 steps:

1. Break down the Project into **Phases** – whatever makes sense for the type of work being undertaken. It could be gathering requirements, designing an office layout or testing a marketing approach.
2. For each Phase, define the required **Outcomes** – define the specific entry and exit criteria for the phase and accommodate each stakeholder need.

3. Use these Outcomes to identify the **Work Products** – specify what is going to be produced, in what format and for whom (a product breakdown structure).
4. Use these Work Products to identify the **Tasks** – break down the work into the manageable chunks necessary to deliver the Work Product.
5. Identify the **dependencies, effort and complexity** of each Task – define any tasks that cannot start or finish until something else (internal or external to the project) has started or finished. Gather the estimates of effort required to complete each task, calibrated by a factor depending on whether it is of high, medium or low complexity.
6. Identify **the resources** (you have or will need) and their **skills/availability** – name the resources (ideally) or skill type and when you are going to need them.
7. **Allocate** these resources to the tasks (a single resource per task is ideal, but if this is not possible, it may be necessary to break the task down further).
8. **Produce** the schedule (work breakdown structure) based on the outputs from Steps 1-7
9. **Compare** this schedule to the delivery targets in the high-level Plan

Repeat until all impacted parties are happy!

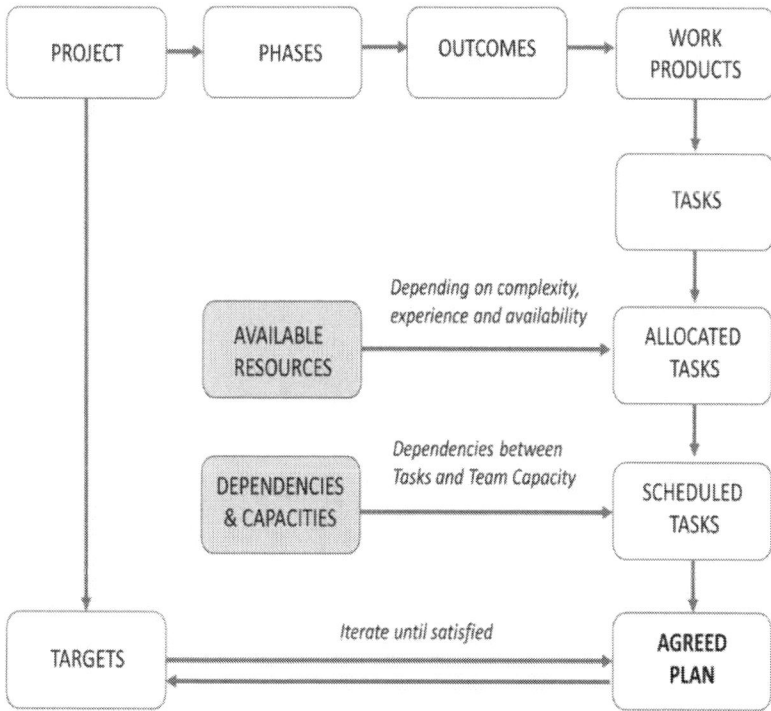

Figure 9.1 – Project Planning 101

9.3 Project Planning in the real world

So, at the very least, these three questions need to be considered:

1. What should plans and schedules look like in these disruptive times?
2. What needs to be done differently?
3. How can they become living documents and not just virtual dust-gatherers in a project folder?

Whatever industry you work in, the word 'agile' is not far from people's lips i.e., the ability to move quickly and easily to keep pace with changing demands. There have been many examples in recent years of companies going out of business due to their inability to recognise the need for change or challenge the status quo.

The way projects are planned and scheduled is no different – in today's world, velocity is king and so plans and schedules need to be fit for this purpose without compromising on quality – a tough call!

'The world is changing very fast. Big will not beat small anymore. It will be the fast beating the slow.' – Rupert Murdoch

The only way to attain market leadership in anything is to only do what you must do to get your product or service out there quickly. Less is more; small is great! It's better to get fast feedback from the early adopters of a new product or service. You will soon know whether you are on the right track.

To achieve this, plans and schedules must allow for continual refinement and not be protected by the aegis of a bureaucratic change management process. Culturally, this is difficult in some organisations who want to see the complete picture up-front but in order to increase the chances of success, this way of working needs to be adopted.

What is needed is Agility, Flexibility, Velocity and Quality.

9.4 Tips **BEFORE** you make your plan

Here are a few considerations before the detailed planning and scheduling starts in earnest: -

Don't eat the entire banquet in one sitting – take a forkful at a time!

Break the work down into small increments, ideally prioritised to deliver the best value to the customer. At the end of each increment, ensure there is something to demonstrate and be prepared to act on the feedback straight away.

Ensure any project partners are working in the same way

This is critical. Selected partners must be able to demonstrate they have the ability to match your delivery timescales and adopt whatever working practices you decide upon. Their milestones must be visible in your plans. This is relevant whether you are manufacturing, marketing, developing a software product, building an extension or anything else really.

Maximise Flow

When scheduling work, try and make sure the person allocated to the task can finish it – ideally by breaking it down into a low level of granularity. In many industries, particularly knowledge work, there is enough data to prove that multi-tasking actually slows down throughput and the higher the utilisation of a resource, the more time it takes to complete a task. So stop starting and start finishing – get it done and then move on to the next item. Queuing will kill you.

Plan to Measure

A wise man once said – 'If you can't measure it then you can't manage it!' Record those vital few measures along the way and calibrate based on coalface experience. This will give you the continuous flow of data you need to improve your estimating process. Always remember that as a general rule in many industries, customers generally prefer predictability to perfection. They'd like both but in these turbulent times, reduction in cycle time from idea to delivery will be their choice, if they are asked to make the call

Plan in Quality

Having said that, reduction in cycle time at any cost will never be acceptable. Quality controls need to be planned in and executed; not taken out when deadlines loom. The key here is fitness for purpose and this will drive the techniques you use. Never leave quality to any testing of the product or service – it will cost you. To paraphrase Steve McConnell in his book *Code Complete* – 'You cannot test in quality – it's like trying to lose weight where the only thing you do is weigh yourself more often'.

Become a Learning Organisation

At the end of every discrete piece of work, get everyone together and review what went well, what didn't go so well and what will be taken forward as an improvement. Learn from any failures and put in countermeasures to preclude their recurrence. Communicate the findings and ensure they are taken on board throughout the organisation.

Plan to do just enough

Unless you are a space agency, this is not rocket science. If you are producing something that will never be used later down the line – challenge it. Keep all your processes and methods as lightweight as possible. Fitness for purpose based on business value and risk should be uppermost in your planning and scheduling sessions.

Plan as a Team

Although Project Managers are responsible for the production and maintenance of the plans and schedules, they cannot possibly do the estimates or ascertain which tasks need to be done first. It requires all representatives in the value chain to drive out the data that will be used to produce the plans - i.e., estimates, priority of requirements, dependencies, risks, constraints and assumptions. Your plan can only ever be your best guess at a point in time – everyone needs to buy in to this.

Minimise Dependencies

One sure-fire way of slowing things down is to have too much reliance on someone or something else, inside or outside of the team, to do something before a task can be started or finished. This is obvious but it's amazing how many plans show the dependencies but don't show any actions to removing them. Even if they cannot be removed on this project, flag them up so something can be done to give follow-on projects a better chance of success.

What's in it for me?

This is where community spirit can be built. Every project will have at least one stakeholder. Many will have significant influence inside the organisation – use these people to your advantage. They will help to get the message across as to why this particular project is so important for the organisation and smooth the path to success. Build a stakeholder map and assign responsibility to the team member who is most likely to build trust and rapport with each impacted party. This type of communication is critical and often gets left behind when the going gets tough – don't let it!

Expect a few failures

There will be some. It took Edison quite a few attempts at getting a light bulb that worked. The same applies to

Henry Ford until his model-T rolled off the production line. The tricks up your sleeve need to ensure that you don't repeat the same mistakes but you do learn from them. Innovation in any environment only comes from experimentation and if you're not making any mistakes, you are not trying hard enough.

Good project managers keep their plans and schedules fluid, open to change based on feedback and with a lightweight level of overhead.

Not so good project managers do the opposite – if it's not working – do more of the same.

9.5 Recap: Planning Fundamentals

Irrespective of the business you are in, any new, amended or to be deleted product or service needs to be planned and the work scheduled. Otherwise it is impossible to demonstrate that the work can get done.

Don't forget to take into account the non-project related activities that your resources will need to do when scheduling tasks – e-mails, presentations, communication sessions, meetings, helping others, training, holidays etc. They will rarely be available 100% of the time on your project.

Use the plan and schedule as living documents. Do a regular review with the team or individual to make sure the plans remain complete and doable. Be prepared to change things as circumstances dictate.

Continue to ensure that you have the people and skills you need – this will require all of your influencing and negotiating skills but escalate if you've tried everything – don't hide things under the carpet.

Avoid adding resources to maintain end dates – it NEVER works – quite the opposite, due to the time it takes to bring new people up to speed (Brooks Law again!)

Remember that the key to when a task can be finished is when it is started. It is very easy to slip the end date – by just one day at a time.

But whatever you do with your plans and schedules, do your level best to: -

- **Keep them simple** – this will come with practice and experimentation
- **Only use fit for purpose processes and methods** – this does not always mean lightweight – it depends on the criticality and risk – tailor to fit.
- **Build that community spirit** – engage your organisation – make everyone feel that this project will be great for them
- **Work as a team** – us and them is best left as a Pink Floyd track! Help the team to do great work, involve them in everything and resolve their issues when they have exhausted every possibility themselves
- **Ignore anybody who says plans and schedules aren't necessary** – just ask them how they know when a project will get done and how? A project without a plan is just a dream; a wish; a bet; a wild stab in the dark.

Finally, at the end of each phase or project, review what went well and not so well and make the data available to the rest of the organisation. It will quickly become an invaluable asset in moving forward within your communities.

'Good judgement comes from experience and a lot of that comes from bad judgement' – *Will Rogers*

Example Business Simulation

The PLAY-IT Business Simulation (described in 14.1) and the CREW Business Simulation (described in 14.4) both allow participants to practice planning work for projects and team members.

10. Team Management

Primary Focus
Primarily Project Team Communities but also Leadership and Target/User Communities.

Key Objectives
Operating a high performing team and assigning the right people in the team to the right tasks at the right time and tracking results - adjusting as required.

Key Chapter Topics
- Effective Team Management
- Managing the Individuals
- Managing the Team
- Team Leadership Self-Assessment
- Example Business Simulation

10.1 Effective Team Management

In Chapter 11 - Team Development, we will describe the steps needed to lay solid foundations for a High Performing Team. Sometimes you will have the luxury of doing this first before you start to manage your team. In other cases, you will have to hit the ground running and fit in team development work wherever you can – almost like re-engineering a Boeing-747 in flight!

There are two key leadership tasks to which you must now assign yourself on an on-going basis - Managing the Individuals and Managing the Team. The key elements of both are shown in Figure 10.1.

We can compare this simplified two-dimensional Team Leadership model with two other very important three-dimensional models.

The first is John Adair's *Action Centred Leadership* model which has as its three dimensions - **Team, Task and Individual**.

The second is a model, credited to James Flaherty in his Coaching book as being inspired by the influential German philosopher Jurgen Habermas and offering its three dimensions of **I, We and It**.

These two models appear quite similar, although the Habermas definition of 'We' encompasses 'Relationships with others' which is wider than Adair's 'Team'.

The two-dimensional Team Leadership model proposed here simplifies things by dropping the Task/IT dimension altogether. The rationale being that much of this work is the responsibility of the team member and not a leadership concern.

However, we attempt to mitigate the effects of this simplification (at least on a relational level) by adding the Customer (relationship) into the 'Managing the Team' dimension.

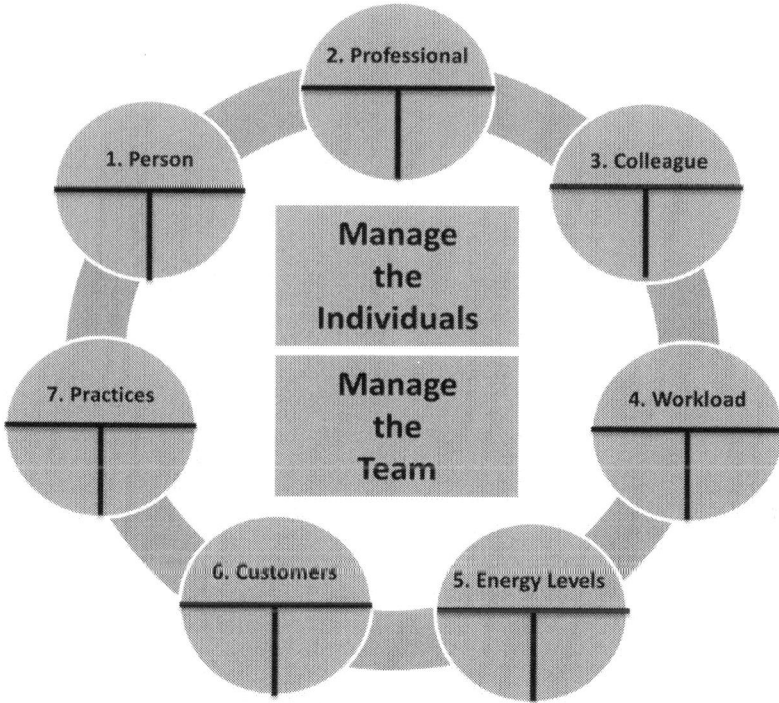

Figure 10.1 – Team Management Responsibilities

10.2 Manage the Individuals

Through your initial change management work, you should now have a much greater insight into your team members. You must continue to build this insight and of course your relationships, which underpin everything.

It's useful to develop the leadership discipline of constantly being able to do a quick "Team Temperature Check' of the people you are responsible for from three different perspectives or lenses.

Task 1: Manage the Person

- What kind of personality do they have?
- In what ways are they different from you?
- What is important to them outside of work?
- What is important to them inside of work?
- What challenges/pressures are they facing at home?
- What challenges/pressures are they facing at work?
- **Are they in an 'OK' place as people?**

Task 2: Manage the Professional

- How good are their job specific skills?
- How strong are their interpersonal skills?
- How good is their leadership/potential?
- What are their strengths and weaknesses?
- How actively are they being developed through training and/or coaching?
- **Are they in an 'OK' place as professionals?**

Task 3: Manage the Colleague

- How do they get on with the other team members?
- Who do they struggle with?
- Who do they work well with?
- What positives and negatives do they bring to team meetings?
- **Are they in an 'OK' place as team members?**

Please refer to Appendix E (Developing Coaching Relationships) for an introduction and further reading on the basics of team member coaching and mentoring.

10.3 Manage the Team

In simple terms, we can add four additional aspects for managing the team:

Task 4: Manage the Team's Workload

It is important to balance the demands coming into the team with the resources available to meet those demands. For each task you will have to decide who should do it, primarily considering their availability, capacity and capability. However, these are not the only points to consider.

You will also need to think about giving people the opportunity to learn by doing tasks which will stretch them – possibly with a more experienced team member acting as a coach / mentor.

You also need to think about boredom i.e., where a task is no longer challenging to an individual. If you keep asking them to do the same thing over and over again, they will get bored, demotivated and may even leave the organisation.

If you are a 'hands-on' project manager, you also need to think about what tasks you specifically pick up. This shows your team that you are not afraid to get your hands dirty.

However, you must be careful to not just select the most interesting or best jobs; or over-schedule yourself as this can be a comfort blanket for a manager who does not feel comfortable with engaging with or looking after their team members.

Task 5: Manage the Team's Energy Levels

It is your job as project manager to look after the people on your team. If you push them too hard then they may become burned out. If you don't push them hard enough then they may become demotivated. You should also be on the lookout for early warning signs of developing problems.

For example, if a colleague has become unusually sullen or irritable, is it because they are feeling the pressure and on their way to a period of stress leave which you could nip in the bud?

Alternatively, if a colleague is starting to take unexplained days off work then they could be applying for other jobs because they are not happy in their work?

On the other hand, if they are not using up their leave or always seeking overtime then this could be pointing at other issues such as financial worries? When did you last review their salaries? What home pressures are they under? Is there a new baby in the family? Has their partner lost their job?

As a project manager, you need to develop effective early people warning systems and be skilful in having conversations with colleagues where you suspect something might be 'off'.

It's an important part of a project manager's job to spot and eliminate any **'barriers or blockers'** which drain team energy levels.

Task 6: Manage the Team's Customers

Your team exists to serve its customers. They can be external or internal customers or a combination of both

A good project manager will develop an awareness of the team's customers and, wherever possible, create direct relationships with them. This can be very helpful as long as it does not appear that you are under-cutting or not trusting your team colleagues.

This is also an important component of your early warning system as it can tell you if projects are going wrong. If you have the right relationships with your customers, they may also give you a quiet 'heads-up' on any people issues.

Task 7: Manage the Team's Practices

You need to be constantly looking at the team's processes and practices to see how they could be improved. Don't be fooled into a false sense of security by the fact that you have just introduced new team practices. They can fossilise just like any others. You need to constantly check whether they are still being used, whether they are producing value and in what way they could be improved.

10.4 Team Leadership Self-Assessment

You might want to take this opportunity to conduct a quick assessment against these 7 key tasks.

Step#1 – Self Assessment

Against each of the 7 tasks, estimate what percentage of your <u>working time</u> you allocate to each on a typical week. This is really an assessment of your *priorities* as a project manager. Be interested in how much time you spend in areas not covered by the 7 tasks. What insights can you take from this? Now score yourself against each of the habits in terms of how *effective* you think you are by using a simple four-point scale i.e.,

1 = Less than effective
2 = Satisfactory
3 = Good
4 = Very effective

Step#2 - Peer Assessment
Now meet with a peer in a similar role as you and assess each other. Where does your colleague reach different conclusions about your effectiveness? What insights can you take from this?

Step#3 – Team Assessment
This is the most useful step and the one which requires the most courage in a leader! Ask your team members to do their honest assessments of you on both time and effectiveness. Make them anonymous and prepare a summary showing your average, highest and lowest scores for each habit? Present the results back to your team and invite comment. What insights can you take from this?

If you would like a free copy of the supporting **Team Leadership/Project Management Assessment Spreadsheet** please email us at
info@dashboardsimulations.com

Example Business Simulation

The CREW Business Simulation (described in 14.4) allows participants to practice managing the work, team and personal aspects of a small project team.

Further Reading
For a more detailed exploration of team development and management see "A Systematic Guide to High Performing Teams" by Ken Thompson, December 2015.

11.   Team Development

Primary Focus
Project Team Communities

Key Objectives
Creating a high performing team to successfully deliver the project.

Key Chapter Topics
- High Performing Team Models
- Team Process Development
- Conducting a Team Process Health Check
- Team Change Management
- Creating a viable project team in a hurry!
- Example Business Simulation

11.1 High Performing Team Models

To enable us to properly look at what is involved in creating a High Performing Team (HPT), there is an important framing question we first need to consider:

Q: Is the creation of a HPT a "change management" project or a "process development" project?

Answer: Yes!

To create a great team, you need to perform "change management" work with the individual team members and "process development" work with the team as a whole. If you neglect the process development work, you will quickly undo the results of your change management work.

For example, poorly run team meetings will rapidly drain any enthusiasm you have cultivated in team members through your careful change management interventions. Likewise, if you neglect the change management work with individuals, the job of creating improved team processes in isolation will be a tedious and somewhat academic exercise, with no real benefits gained.

An analogy would be a racing driver (change management) and their racing car (process development). To win races, you need excellence in both the driver and the car (although it seems that great drivers racing average cars is nearly always a better proposition than average drivers racing great cars!)

In Figure 11.1, we propose a practical integrated framework for High Performing Teams which will help you identify and contextualise the main priorities for both team process development and team change management. It is crucial that you address both these aspects of team development as no team can achieve high performance on process or change in isolation.

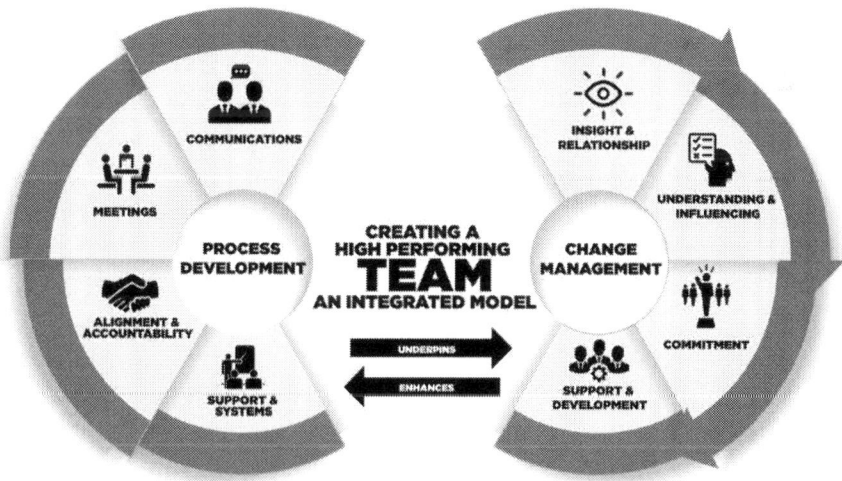

Figure 11.1 – Integrated HPT Model

11.2 Team Process Development

There are four areas of process which are fundamental to successful teams:

1. Meetings
2. Alignment and Accountability
3. Communications
4. Support and Systems

These areas are of broadly equal importance and can be thought of as four legs of a stool – if any one of them is deficient, the stool will be unstable and not fit for purpose.

We can expand each of these areas further into 16 specific processes / practices (four per process area):

1. <u>Team Meetings</u>

M1: Operational Meetings
Ensure that team operational meetings are regular and effective.

M2: Strategy / Problem-Solving Meetings
Ensure that any team strategy/problem solving meetings are timely and effective.

M3: Relationship / Trust Meetings
Ensure that team meetings to build relationships/trust are timely and effective.

M4: Virtual Meeting/Phone Meeting Practices
Ensure that the team is able to conduct effective meetings in person or remotely/virtually.

2. Team Alignment & Accountability

A1: Team Ground Rules
Ensure that the team has defined what constitutes acceptable and unacceptable behaviours.

A2: Team Goals & Objectives
Ensure that the team has clearly defined and communicated mutual goals and have agreed how changes to these are communicated.

A3: Team Member Accountabilities
Ensure that each team member has clearly defined accountabilities within the team.

A4: Team Leadership Roles
Ensure that, in addition to the project manager, the team enables supporting team leadership roles.

3. Team Communications

C1: Open Communications Practices
Ensure that team members have an environment for openness with both the project manager and their colleagues.

C2: Conflict Resolution Process
Ensure the team has processes to quickly and effectively address interpersonal conflict.

C3: Decision-Making Practices
Ensure the team uses recognised decision-making techniques appropriate to different situations.

C4: Information-sharing
Ensure that the team effectively shares accountabilities, priorities, updates and information.

4. <u>Team Support & Systems</u>

S1: Personal Development
Ensure each team member has an up-to-date personal development plan in place.

S2: Coaching Relationships
Ensure project manager(s) regularly participate in coaching conversations with other team members.

S3: Peer Support System
Ensure team members directly support and help each other through collaboration.

S4: Early Warning System
Ensure team members keep a lookout for any risks which might impact any other team member's ability to deliver their results.

11.3 Conducting a Team Process Health Check

However, there are two very important questions you need to address before attempting to implement these processes in a team:

Q1: How do you establish which processes are the most important for your team?

Q2: Are the process priorities the same for all teams?

Let's start with the second question first. All teams start in a different place in terms of capability. Your first job as a project manager/team builder is to conduct a team process "health check" against the team process framework. This will establish, for each of the 16 processes, whether an existing process exists, to what extent it is being used and to what extent it is working.

So, as all teams start off with a different process capability profile, you should generally prioritise those processes which are either absent or broken before you try to improve those which are already in place and working to varying degrees.

However, this is not the whole story as some team processes are more important than others. For example, if a regular team operational meeting is badly broken, this will damage a team every single week. Whereas, if a team relationship meeting is broken, this might only damage a team once a month or once a quarter.

It can be useful to group your team processes into three levels of team importance/maturity with the suggestion that you address the level 1 process issues before you address the level 2 process issues and move on to Level 3. Walk before you run!

LEVEL 3
Advanced Processes (7)

LEVEL 2
Key Processes (5)

LEVEL 1
Foundation Processes (4)

This will allow you to create "basecamps" of process maturity as you climb the high performing team "mountain" and reduces the risk of creating "improvement chaos" within your team.

In figure 11.2, we suggest a generic sequence for improving the 16 team processes. Please bear in mind this is not intended to be prescriptive, but rather a guide.

For example, we consider the four most important team processes that need to be addressed as:

- Team operational meetings
- Team ground rules
- Open communications
- Peer support system

	>> LEVEL 1 >>	>> LEVEL 2 >>	>> LEVEL 3 >>
MEETINGS	Operational Meetings		
			Strategy/Problem-Solving Meetings
			Relationship/Trust Meetings
		Virtual/Phone Meeting Practices	
ALIGNMENT	Team Ground Rules		
		Team Goals & Objectives	
		Team Member Accountabilities	
			Team Leadership Roles
COMMS	Open Communications		
		Conflict Resolution Process	
			Decision-Making Practices
			Information-sharing
SUPPORT			Personal Development
		Coaching Relationships	
	Peer Support System		
			Early Warning System

Figure 11.2 – Team Process Maturity Model

Figure 11.3 is a screenshot from a Microsoft Excel Spreadsheet which you can use to do a Team Process Health Check. It allows you to assess each of the 16 process elements on a scale of 0-3 ranging from totally absent to present and effective. The results are shown graphically as a bar chart (summary level) and a spider diagram (detailed level).

The spreadsheet also allows you to record your action priority (1-3) for each of the 16 process elements, which it then compares automatically with the three-stage process maturity model described earlier. This will give you a good indication of whether your proposed sequence of process improvements makes sense in terms of relative process importance.

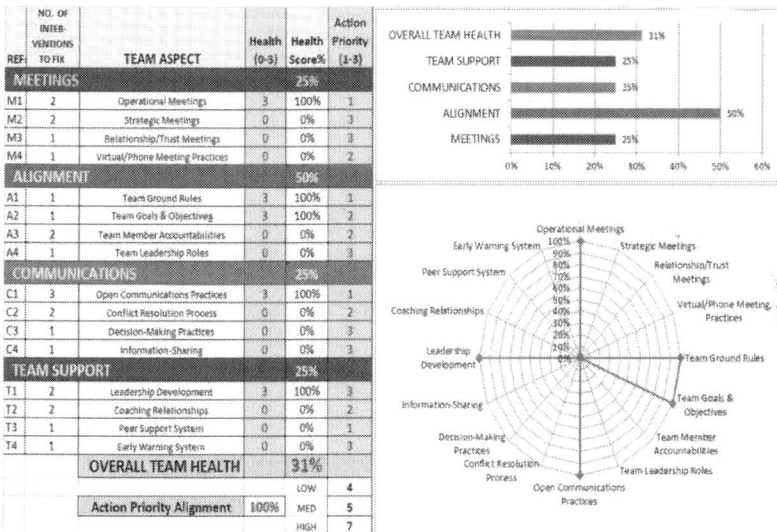

REF	NO. OF INTER-VENTIONS TO FIX	TEAM ASPECT	Health (0-3)	Health Score%	Action Priority (1-3)
MEETINGS				25%	
M1	2	Operational Meetings	3	100%	1
M2	2	Strategic Meetings	0	0%	3
M3	1	Relationship/Trust Meetings	0	0%	3
M4	1	Virtual/Phone Meeting Practices	0	0%	2
ALIGNMENT				50%	
A1	1	Team Ground Rules	3	100%	1
A2	1	Team Goals & Objectives	3	100%	2
A3	2	Team Member Accountabilities	0	0%	2
A4	1	Team Leadership Roles	0	0%	3
COMMUNICATIONS				25%	
C1	3	Open Communications Practices	3	100%	1
C2	2	Conflict Resolution Process	0	0%	2
C3	1	Decision-Making Practices	0	0%	3
C4	1	Information-Sharing	0	0%	3
TEAM SUPPORT				25%	
T1	2	Leadership Development	3	100%	3
T2	2	Coaching Relationships	0	0%	2
T3	1	Peer Support System	0	0%	1
T4	1	Early Warning System	0	0%	3
		OVERALL TEAM HEALTH		31%	
		Action Priority Alignment	100%	LOW	4
				MED	5
				HIGH	7

OVERALL TEAM HEALTH — 31%
TEAM SUPPORT — 25%
COMMUNICATIONS — 25%
ALIGNMENT — 50%
MEETINGS — 25%

Figure 11.3 – Team Process Health Check

If you would like a free copy of the **Team Process Health Check Spreadsheet** please email us at info@dashboardsimulations.com

11.4 Team Change Management

The second aspect of creating a high performing team is the individual change management initiatives with each of its members.

Here you should employ the same principles and practices that were identified for senior leaders and described in Chapter 4 - Stakeholder Engagement.

11.5 Creating a viable project team in a hurry!

Please refer to Appendix C – High Speed Project Teams - for some practical tips on this surprisingly frequent scenario that project managers find themselves facing in today's fast-paced business world.

Example Business Simulation

The CHAPTER Business Simulation (described in 14.6) allows participants to address the challenge of establishing a high performing team through team member change management and team process development.

Further Reading

For a more detailed exploration of team development and management see "A Systematic Guide to High Performing Teams" by Ken Thompson, December 2015.

12.   Partner Engagement

Primary Focus
Project Team Communities

Key Objectives
Developing strong collaborative relationships with key external parties that are needed for successful project delivery.

Key Chapter Topics
*   The need for Project Partners
*   Identifying potential partners
*   Partner Engagement
*   Partnership Ground Rules
*   Conflict Management
*   Partnerships should be "SAFE"
*   Example Business Simulation

12.1 The need for Project Partners

Project Managers rarely have direct control of all the resources they need to deliver a project. If this is the case and to deliver a successful outcome, it will be necessary to call on individuals and teams outside of the core team.

With proper planning, it should be possible to identify these needs in advance and get everything in place - planned, agreed and scheduled.

However, no matter how good your planning is, there will always be other unforeseen needs which emerge, some of which may be really urgent. This is where you will need to rely on the relationships you have (or have not built) with your external partners.

Michael J. Cunningham, in his 2002 book "Partners.com", identifies seven main reasons why organisations create partnerships or alliances:

- financial reasons

- market share

- control of costs

- shorter time to market

- entry to new or adjacent markets

- sustainable competitive advantage

- competitive pressure

However, in our context, we are more interested in partnerships between teams and between individuals within organisations rather than between different organisations. Therefore we can simplify the reasons for partnerships as follows:

1. To increase the chances of a successful project delivery

2. To provide a higher value proposition to the ultimate project customers

3. To enable the project to be delivered faster or cheaper or with less resources

In a sense points 2 and 3 are really elaborations of point 1.

Note: *Having said that, we should not necessarily restrict our partnering focus just to those inside our own organisation or to just technical partners. External parties and non-technical partners may also be essential to our project.*

12.2 Identifying potential partners

One of the most effective techniques for identifying the need for partnerships is the plain old-fashioned SWOT Matrix (Strengths, Weaknesses, Opportunities and Threats).

Firstly, you should conduct it for your own team in terms of your aspirations for the project. The Weaknesses and Threats identified will be the starting point to consider partnerships.

In his book, "The Networked Enterprise", Ken developed another technique, **Synergy Discovery**, albeit aimed more at partnership building between independent companies. Instead of starting with a SWOT analysis, the different partner roles in a potential project or venture are considered from the perspective of what unique values each party might bring to the project.

This technique can be readily adapted for internal alliancing by identifying the key partner roles needed to be successful in the proposed project. In the book, Ken suggests the following six roles, which can easily be adapted for partnerships within the same organisation:

- *Core Service or Product Provider* (can be multiple)

- *Channel to Market* (in an internal context, this could be the partner who manages the stakeholder and customer relationships)

- *Innovator* (in an internal context, this could be a partner who adds something special or unique)

- *Supporting Provider* (can be multiple)

- *Integrator* (in an internal context, this could be the partner who is responsible for pulling all the work streams together and making sure they interlock properly)

- *Investor* (in an internal context, this could be the partner who puts together the business case with an attractive return on investment and ensures the benefits are realised).

In the remainder of this section, we will explore the following three vital alliancing disciplines:

- **Partner Engagement:** how and with whom do you start a partnership conversation?

- **Ground Rules**: how do you make a partnership agreement work in practice?

- **Conflict Management**: what can you do when things start to go wrong?

12.3 Partner Engagement

To build an partnership you will need to engage with somebody from within the potential partner organisation. You may already know the right person but what if you don't? Who should you choose? A powerful technique you can use here is the Simple Stakeholder Map (Figure 4.1) described in Chapter 4.

Once you have identified the right individual, you can apply the principles of individual engagement described within.

12.4 Partnership Ground Rules

Whilst it is relatively easy to make high-level partnership agreements, putting them into practice is far more challenging.

There are 3 common extremes:

- Leave things vague - to be addressed as each issue arises

- Document the agreement prescriptively but in too much detail

- Fixate on the legal / contractual view of the partnership

From experience, what works best is some middle ground based on the creation and agreement of a simple 1-page set of **Ground Rules.** These simply and concisely answer the following key questions between two or more partners:

1. What leadership roles will we have and who will perform these roles?

2. What behaviours or actions would damage or destroy the partnership?

3. What are the main potential conflict of interest areas and how will any issues arising be addressed?

4. What will be the level of transparency and information sharing between partners?

5. What is the protocol for resolving partner issues and disputes (see 12.5 - Conflict Management)?

6. How often will we meet as partners, who will be involved and for what purpose?

7. How will the partners communicate with each other outside of meetings?

8. What commitments will the partners make to each other to support, respect and/or enhance their respective reputations with key stakeholders?

The final point is particularly important for the spirit of partnership, to ensure that one party does not take all the credit and make the other look like a "lame duck".

It is better to start by answering these eight questions first and only then extending the agreement as required, rather than trying to identify and answer every eventuality upfront.

12.5 Conflict Management

Things rarely proceed exactly as planned in a partnership relationship. There are two common problems – *genuine misunderstandings* and *boundary testing*.

Common misunderstandings are where both sides look at an action of the other party, make interpretations around motive and then start acting on these conclusions. Consequently, the other party makes their own interpretations and the ensuing actions can rapidly poison the relationship. Usually these interpretations of motive are not shared with the other party.

The solution here is to spot early on that you have entered the genuine misunderstandings zone and have a conversation with the other party about it in a spirit of curiosity and respectfulness, rather than blame and point scoring.

A useful device here is the so-called *Ladder of Inference*, shown in figure 12.1, which can chart the journey from a single observation to vastly different interpretations. The first rung starts with making observations from which we select certain data. We then add meanings and assumptions in order to reach conclusions which become beliefs and lead us to take actions.

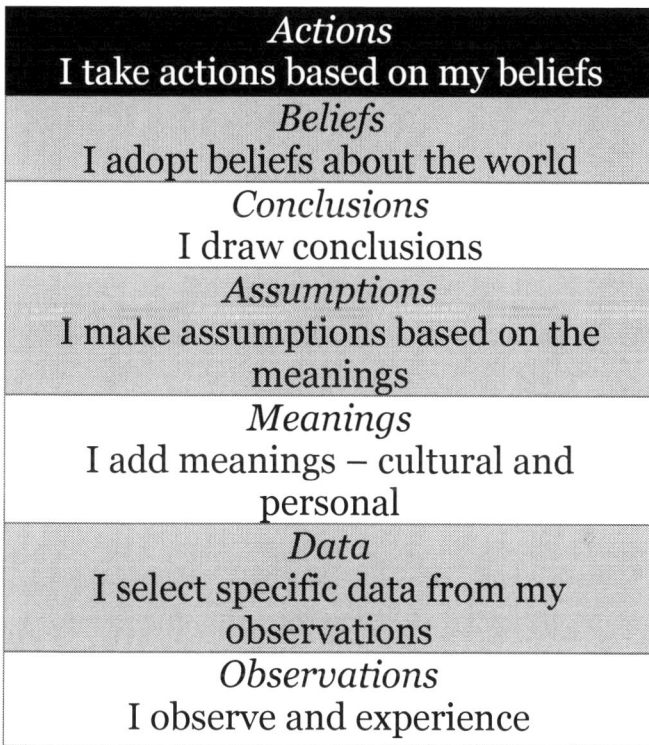

Actions   I take actions based on my beliefs
Beliefs   I adopt beliefs about the world
Conclusions   I draw conclusions
Assumptions   I make assumptions based on the meanings
Meanings   I add meanings – cultural and personal
Data   I select specific data from my observations
Observations   I observe and experience

Figure 12.1 - The Ladder of Inference

The ladder can be used to clarify how we have suddenly jumped to certain *automatic* conclusions. It is highly effective if your "ladder" can be shared with the other party, who should also be invited to construct their own version – all starting with the same shared observation e.g.," You whispered something to your colleague at a critical point in today's meeting with our joint customer."

The conversation may continue along the lines of "this observation led me to believe that you were working against our joint interests. When you hear my conclusion, you would then be able to share with me that you were only reminding your colleague that you would have to leave the meeting very promptly to pick up your daughter as the school had just sent you a text to say she had been feeling unwell."

Boundary Testing is very different from genuine misunderstandings and occurs when one party in a partnership acts in a certain way for selfish reasons or to test the limits of the agreement. Boundary Testing happens all the time in partnerships, once the honeymoon period ends!

Relatively recent research has proven that a strategy known as Tit for Tat (TfT) is the best one to adopt for long-term sustainable cooperation and is also a great way to respond to boundary testing.

However, most teams have never heard of TfT and either have no strategy or try to play what they call Win-Win, which in practice usually involves one of two approaches:

Mr. Nice Guy

"I will assume you are cooperating with me until it is proven you are not. Then I won't work with you again."

In this situation, you can easily be taken advantage of, as at that point you are often too resentful to try and put it right. Relationships that start with this kind of naivety generally end in tears!

Mr. Stand-Off

"I will assume you are not cooperating until it is proven that you are, and if it is not conclusively proven after a certain time, I will assume (privately) that you are not a good partner."

Relationships that start with this kind of distrust usually become self-fulfilling prophecies. So, start hyper-cautiously and you won't be disappointed!

It can be argued that although Win-Win is a highly desirable outcome/state, it is in itself not the best strategy for getting there. This is because Win-Win (in both guises described above) has no means of challenging a non-cooperating partner and then recovering. Specifically, Win-Win lacks any mechanism for applying *sanctions* to the other party.

On the other hand, TfT is based on four simple principles:

1. Never be the first to defect
2. Retaliate only after your partner has defected
3. Be prepared to forgive after carrying out just one act of retaliation
4. Let the other players know up front that you are operating to these principles

If you find yourself being *boundary tested* and you are confident it is not just a common misunderstanding, you can use TfT to quickly mirror back the offending behaviour, being careful not to escalate or respond disproportionately. Then you forgive and continue to co-operate positively and watch to see what happens next.

If the issue continues, TfT can be used again until it stops or prompts a formal conflict resolution discussion using the approach you agreed in Point 5 of the Ground Rules detailed in 12.4.

12.6 Partnerships should be "SAFE"

In Ken's book "The Networked Enterprise", he describes what he learnt from establishing about a dozen business networks and other collaborative ventures.

Based on this experience, he realised that there are four vital ingredients needed in any partnership - Synergy, Appetite, Feasibility and Economics. If you lack any one of these four **SAFE Factors,** then the partnership is unlikely to work for all the parties.

S is for SYNERGY
Is there genuine synergy between the parties? If you all do the same thing or do things which are too diverse to join up, then you don't have Synergy.

A is for APPETITE
If there is Synergy, do the parties actually want to partner? If Synergy is the *mind* of alliancing, then Appetite is its *heart*. You can't have viable partnerships without Appetite.

F is for FEASIBILILTY
OK, so there might be Synergy and Appetite but if it requires a monumental effort to partner or there are huge practical obstacles, then it won't happen. Is this partnership actually Feasible?

E is for ECONOMICS
Finally, your proposed partnership may well have ticked the other three boxes but unless there are some clear

concrete and timely financial benefits for all the parties i.e., Economics, then any partnership is unlikely to be sustainable.

Example Business Simulation

The FUSION Business Simulation (described in 14.2) allows participants to collaborate between teams to ensure both team and overall goals are achieved.

Further Reading

For a more detailed exploration of partner engagement see "A Systematic Guide to Collaboration and Competition within Organizations" by Ken Thompson, March 2017.

13. Business Simulations for Learning

Key Objectives
The rationale, benefits, examples and best practices in the use of business simulations for effective blended learning on project management.

Key Chapter Topics
- Management Development Simulations
- Rationale for Learning via Simulation
- Benefits of Learning through Simulation
- Seven Defining Characteristics of Simulations
- Project Management Simulations for Learning

13.1 Management Development Simulations

In this chapter, we want to introduce Business Simulations which are used for Management and Leadership Development. Our focus on management and leadership does exclude very useful simulations which are used to develop general or specialised practitioner skills such as customer service or servicing a computer printer. We also exclude other types of valuable (and sometimes life-saving) simulations, such as those used for analytics, medical skills development or other operational skills (which tend to require hyper-realistic simulation models).

We will also offer some guidance on their use for Project Management. Note that we have ended many of the chapters in this book with a reference to a business simulation which is particularly relevant to the key topics described in that chapter (see Chapter 14 for more details).

13.2 Rationale for Learning via Simulation

There are four main reasons why Business Simulations are chosen for learning:

1. *Simulations Provide a Safe and Efficient Learning Environment*

"Let's take flight simulation as an example. If you're trying to train a pilot, you can simulate almost the whole course. You don't have to get in an airplane until late in the process." - Roy Romer

Business Simulation owes a huge debt to the techniques pioneered in aviation flight simulation (generally also hyper-realistic). In commercial aviation, flight simulation is used extensively in three main areas – Skills Training, Emergency Procedures and Type Conversation with the three main benefits being safety, costs and environmental impact.

In his white paper "What Business Simulation designers can learn from Aviation Flight Simulation", Ken explores how these applications and benefits also apply perfectly to the use of business simulations for learning.

2. *Simulations combine Experiential and Social Learning*

Business simulations are great tools for learning by doing and gaining insight by making mistakes. This is classic experiential learning. Team-based business simulations and facilitated simulations add that extra dimension of being able to share those learning experiences with others.

Jay Cross, in his excellent book, "Informal Learning: Rediscovering the Natural Pathways That Inspire Innovation and Performance", establishes that up to 90%

of the information and skills we need to do our jobs is learned in this way rather than formally, using what he refers to as Informal or Social Learning.

3. *Simulations exploit Gamification Techniques to make learning more engaging*

"Gamification" is defined as the application of gaming techniques in non-gaming applications. If done thoughtfully, adding gaming elements to business simulations (such as leader boards, penalties, rewards and the unexpected), can significantly enhance engagement and team cohesion through competition with other teams.

4. *Simulations offer the potential for Scalable Engagement*

Facilitated sessions not involving simulation can be hugely effective but are often difficult to scale as they are very dependent on the facilitators and can be very labour-intensive. On the other hand, technology such as e-learning can be quite easy to scale but very difficult to create real engagement in the participants.

Business simulations can provide the best of both worlds - Scalable Engagement - where the same sessions can be rolled out quickly and effectively to hundreds of managers or leaders.

13.3 Benefits of Learning through Simulation

When we interview game participants or business sponsors after business simulation events, the benefits they consistently report fall into five categories:

1. *Virtual Experience*

This is the classic flight simulator learning model where participants get to try out 'dangerous things' in a safe and forgiving environment, with no adverse business consequences. 'Virtual Experience' not only involves the important decision-making which participants can practice but also the scenarios they may encounter.

There are also the major and minor unexpected 'shocks' to be considered which the participants have either brought on themselves or which have been pre-programmed into the simulation, outside of their control.

2. *Knowledge Sharing*

A well-designed simulation game is one of the most effective ways for organisations to disseminate and spread knowledge, experience and best practice between colleagues using the social and informal learning approaches highlighted earlier in this chapter.

3. *Resolving Dilemmas*

Any well-designed simulation should present the participants with dilemmas. These can come in many forms and include business, leadership and team dilemmas.

Simulation games should reflect the real-world scarcities that there are rarely enough resources (such as money, people, machinery and stock) to achieve everything you would like to achieve, and therefore trade-offs must be made.

4. *Change and Pressure (Agility)*

As well as having to address dilemmas and scarcities, a simulation can also model the real-world situation that things are always changing unexpectedly and that there is always a time pressure factor. This is very much the essence of 'agility' – the ability to handle unexpected change well and in a timely manner.

5. *Confidence and Ambition*

Finally, a common theme reported by simulation participants 3-6 months after an event, is that they feel more confident and are taking on bigger responsibilities in their jobs/roles. When we ask 'Why', a common response is that the simulation they played was challenging yet they still succeeded (for example, running a flour mill or a country business unit in the face of challenging trading and market conditions).

13.4 Seven Defining Characteristics of Simulations

There are many different characteristics of business simulations for learning but the following seven properties definitively classify these types:

1. **Players:** Are the simulation participants playing as individuals or playing as teams?

For example, in the CREW Team Management simulation (see 14.4), the players normally engage with the simulation as teams.

2. **Player Dynamic:** Are the simulation players collaborating, competing or some combination of the two?

In our simulation for Inter-departmental Communications (FUSION – See 14.2)), the teams start off by competing for scarce resources to achieve their own goals but end up collaborating and then achieve higher level goals.

3. **Role of the Computer:** Are the simulation participants playing against the computer or playing against each other?

For example, we have a Business Acumen simulation (XSIM) where all teams grow market share independently of each other but in our other Business Acumen simulation (COMPETE), the players or teams compete directly for market share in real-time.

Note: Please go to our website - www.dashboardsimulations.com for further details on XSIM and COMPETE

4. **Learning Domains:** What are the main management/leadership topics that the simulation addresses?

Typically, there will be 1-3 primary domains and 1-2 secondary domains. Any more than this is usually a sign of an overly-complex simulation or an unrealistic set of learning objectives.

5. **Mediation:** How is the learning simulation mediated – is it player self-directed or facilitated by a person or even by the computer as a virtual simulator?

For example, CHAPTER - High Performing Team Simulation (See 14.6) can be played in self-directed mode (as an individual or team) with the Virtual Insights switched ON or with a human facilitator and the Virtual Insights switched OFF.

6. **Customisation:** Is the simulation off-the-shelf or custom-built? If it is off-the-shelf, can it be configured? If it is custom-built, is it built from scratch or based on existing simulation components?

For example, the SPAR WARS simulation was built from scratch for a major convenience store client but COMPETE is an off-the-shelf simulation that can be substantially configured for a client without any coding being required.

NOTE: Please go to our website – www.dashboardsimulations.com for further details on SPAR WARS and COMPETE

7. **Off-Sim Elements**: Is the simulation wrapped up in some off-sim components such as papers, props, role

plays or even actors or is the simulation in itself, the entire learning experience?

Off-sim components, if designed and implemented well, can greatly enhance the whole "blended learning experience". In a simulation such as COHORT (See 14.3), the in-simulation characters can also be role-played by the facilitator or by actors.

13.5 Project Management Simulations for Learning

Sadly, in our experience, no single business simulation or game can do justice to all 12 aspects of the Project Management Model (see figure 13.1). You really need to decide what the most important aspects of "Project Management" are for each particular learning situation.

Even if a simulation covered all of the topics in this book, it would probably be quite a one-dimensional learning experience. What we recommend, consistent with best practices in Blended Learning, is to pick a simulation which covers the highest priority project management topics and to complement it using role-plays and off-sim exercises to address the other less critical project topics for the particular situation.

Therefore, referring to the Project Management model

A Community Perspective on Project Management: 12 key disciplines for success			
COMMUNITIES	**LEADER**	**TARGET**	**PROJECT**
Internal	Sponsors	Influencers	Core Team
+	+	+	+
External	Stakeholders	End Users	Partners
PROJECT	1. Business Planning + 2. Benefits Realisation	5. Monitoring, Measuring & Correcting + 6. Commitment Management	9. Planning & Scheduling + 10. Team Management
CHANGE	3. Sponsor Communications + 4. Stakeholder Engagement	7. Word of Mouth + 8. User Adoption	11. Team Development + 12. Partner Engagement

Figure 13.1 - Project Management Tasks Model

If your focus is mostly on the Project Team dimension of the Project Management model, you might consider simulations like CREW (14.4), CHAPTER (14.6) or FUSION (14.2).

If your focus is mostly on the Target/User aspect of the Project Management model, you might consider simulations like SPREAD (14.5) or PLAY-IT (14.1).

If your focus is mostly on the Leader/Business aspect of the Project Management model, you might consider simulations like COHORT (14.3).

Chapter 14 - Project Management Simulations - provides an overview of each of these six simulations.

Further Reading

For a more detailed exploration of business simulations and business games for leadership and management see "A Systematic Guide to Game-Based Learning (GBL) in Organizational Teams" by Ken Thompson, January 2016.

14. Project Management Simulations

<u>Key Objectives</u>
Introducing examples of different types of business simulations which can be used to develop skills in various aspects of project management.

<u>Key Chapter Topics</u>
- Major Projects/Support Simulation
- Inter Team Collaboration Simulation
- Change Management Simulation
- Work & Team Management Simulation
- Project Roll-out Simulation
- Team Formation Simulation

14.1 PLAY-IT Major Projects/Support Simulation

Overview
In the PLAY-IT simulation, participants become the leadership teams of a Global IT function for a one-year period divided into four quarters. Before they start the simulation, the participants are given information about potential technology projects which Global IT could conduct for the benefit of its 100,000 internal users. The participants also receive new and updated information about these projects at the start of each quarter of the simulation.

The goal is to select and execute projects which provide the maximum return and satisfaction for the enterprise's internal customers and to manage these projects with professionalism and commercial awareness.

Each quarter, teams must make the following decisions for each project they choose:

- Whether to start the project and Why
- The best way to execute the project in terms of the different options – (technical / geographical / commercial)
- How much to recover in project costs from internal customers through internal charges
- When and How to schedule, resource and manage the project throughout its full lifecycle

The Global IT department used in the simulation is a small function starting with just six multi-skilled staff but acquiring a new staff member each quarter taking headcount up to nine staff by the final quarter. Teams must work within strict resourcing constraints and are NOT permitted to hire or buy in more resources.

Simulation Learning Objectives
To enable participants to enhance their skills experientially and socially in key areas by engaging in an intensive team business simulation played competitively under time pressure.

They will need to:

- Optimise the use of scarce resources
- Manage Risks
- Display agility when the unexpected happens
- Put a Customer/Business perspective on technology
- Demonstrate Leadership in technology
- Exemplify great teamwork and individual style

Simulation Decisions

In each round, teams must decide which new projects to start and the level of resourcing that must continue to be applied to projects that were started in previous rounds.

As well as deciding whether to start a project, the teams must also select the best technical option. A project may also switch to a different technical option at the start of a new quarter, in which case there may be a predefined switching cost - a one-off charge required to close the previous option.

In addition, the start-up costs for the new option may or may not need to be repeated. This will depend on whether the switch is considered to be a "Major Switch", in which case teams must restart from zero as existing adopted users cannot be carried forward into different technologies.

Likewise, some switches may not make good business sense and will be penalised financially in the simulation.

Teams must also decide how much is appropriate and fair to recover from users for the upfront project costs that the Global IT function have incurred to implement the solution.

Finally, teams must decide how much of their limited resources to apply to each project in terms of these four categories:

- Evaluation/Approval
- Communications /Change Management
- Delivery/User Support
- Localisation

The team decision entry screen for any of the 4 projects in the simulation is shown in Figure 14.1.1:

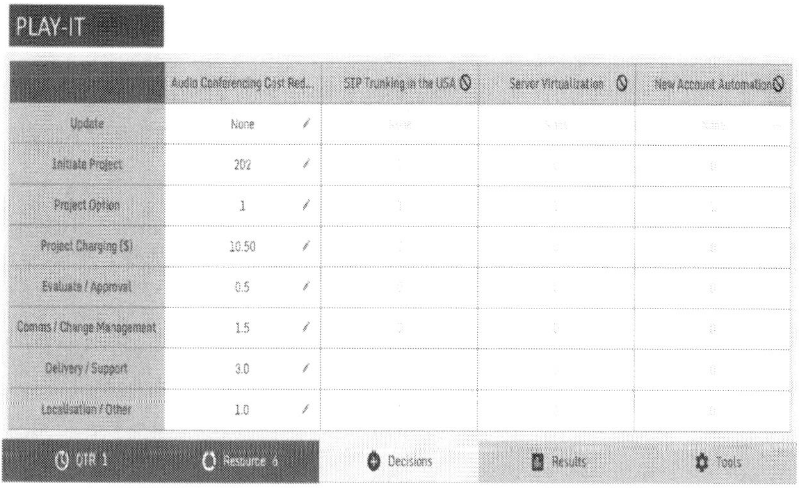

Figure 14.1.1 - PLAY-IT Decisions Screen

Key Simulation rules and logic

- Team decisions drive user adoption levels for each project as consequently these will drive both financial and non-financial results (e.g., customer satisfaction).
- Teams decide quarterly resourcing levels in terms of FTEs (full time equivalents). These may be fractional (e.g. 1.5). Resource decisions are compared with the optimum resourcing needs for the project during the period (derived from the project briefings) and with total resources available across all projects.
- Teams have unlimited financial budgets in terms of both Capital Expenses (CAPEX) and Operating Expenses (OPEX).
- Payback period for all projects is one year and all projects should be fully completed in this timeframe.
- Each project may have all or any of the following costs: one-off (capital) cost, quarterly recurring cost (e.g. license per-user cost), extra resourcing costs (currently not permitted) and switching costs. These different project cost elements can be incurred either by Global IT or the end users themselves.
- Once a project has started, it cannot be stopped. A team may choose not to apply any further resources but will still incur costs and benefits. Once any project is "fully adopted" (> 90%), it needs to be supported by Global IT at an ongoing level of 0.5 FTE per quarter.
- Customer Satisfaction has two components – Value Perception and Adoption Level. If satisfaction drops below a certain threshold in any quarter, this will have a negative impact on the next quarter's

adoption. In addition, once "Full Adoption" (>90%) is achieved on a project, Customer Satisfaction will depend on the resourcing levels for support.

• Value Perception depends on a comparison by the user of any User Charges with a Perceived Cost Benchmark of comparable, externally sourced services. If User Charges are set too high, this will impact Customer Satisfaction levels which could impact subsequent user adoption. If charges are set too low, then costs will not be fully recovered.

Simulation Dashboards

A screenshot from of the main simulation dashboard is shown in figure 14.1.2. It shows key indicators such as User Adoption, Satisfaction, Resourcing, Return on Investment (RoI) and Cost Recoveries.

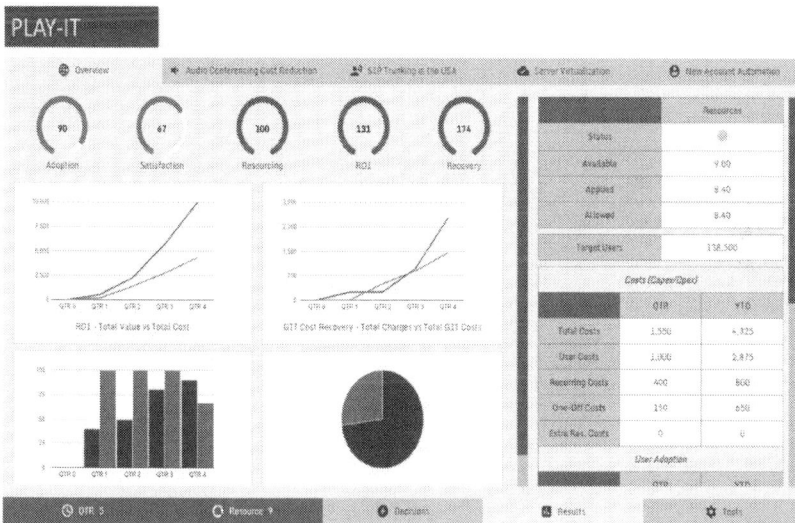

Figure 14.1.2 - PLAY-IT Results Screen

More details on PLAY-IT can be found at:
www.dashboardsimulations.com

14.2 FUSION Inter Team Collaboration Simulation

FUSION is a competitive Collaboration game involving four departments who attempt to achieve both their departmental and organisational goals as they trade limited resources from a shared pool.

14.2.1 - FUSION Results Screen

Two of the teams are mostly (but not exclusively) consumers of resources, the other two being mostly (but not exclusively) suppliers of resources. In each of the three rounds, there are not quite enough resources to go round and teams face the challenge of trying to meet their team/departmental goals but not at the expense of the greater organisation represented by the four 4 teams.

The teams, as a collective, must also avoid penalties for bad business practices such as committing to supply resources which they do not have or failing to achieve adequate resourcing levels to complete their minimum essential work in a period.

The FUSION game is essentially a collaboration scenario but with a competitive edge because no team wants to come out worse than all the others in terms of over-sacrificing its specific departmental objectives for the greater good. This kind of scenario is so endemic in organisations that it has a name – "Sub-Optimisation" – the intense desire of sub-units to achieve individual goals which can result in overall organisational performance being less than it might be – i.e., 'sub-optimal.'

For more on this important topic see "Optimizing Each Part of a Firm Doesn't Optimize the Whole Firm" by Greg Satell in the Harvard Business Review, January 2016

One of the most engaged parts of FUSION is the inter-team negotiations during each round, which can also be used to teach the 'principled negotiation' skills described earlier in Chapter 3.

Specifically:
- Resource providers must try and meet the demands of their resource consumer colleagues but without committing more resources than they can secure.
- Resource consumers need to try and live within the constraints of the resource provider colleagues but being very careful not to settle for less resources than they need to perform their basic jobs.
- Resource providers and suppliers need to collaborate in lobbying and negotiating with programme and line management to make the case for extra unbudgeted resources, if they feel the overall big picture aims will be compromised without them.

FUSION is deceptively simple and can be played in three hours by up to 50 people, organised within four teams.

An important part of FUSION is monitoring and enforcing a set of agreed game protocols:

1. Teams should complete their decision forms and place them in the simulation box before the buzzer sounds at the end of each round. Late forms will result in a null return for the team, for that particular round.

2. Team decision input forms are confidential to each team and should not leave the team tables or be shown to any other team. Teams can talk to other teams only in terms of the resources they need or intend to provide to other teams.

3. Teams should use normal business language in all conversations (no use of the words "scores" or "goals" or "simulation").

4. Teams should honour the agreements they make with other teams – back-stabbing other teams is not part of the simulation.

5. Conversations between teams should be seated and semi-formal between nominated representatives and with a facilitator present. Only two teams should be represented in any meeting unless agreed with the facilitator in advance.

6. Facilitators will give one warning of any potential first protocol violation (Yellow Card). If the violation continues or is repeated, the facilitator will allocate a penalty to the team via their team assessment score (Red Card).

More details on FUSION can be found at:
www.dashboardsimulations.com

14.3 COHORT Change Management Simulation

COHORT is a computer-based business simulation game designed specifically to illustrate the concepts discussed in this book.

Specifically, the simulation allows leaders and managers, playing in teams against their colleagues, to practice their change management influencing skills in a safe environment.

At the start of the simulation, the participants analyse the briefing material on the target organisation, which can either be totally fictitious or similar to their own.

14.3.1 – COHORT Decisions Screen

Players must choose carefully which interventions to make with each stakeholder member by considering three key factors:

- Their *attitude* to the proposed change (supporting, neutral or opposing)
- Their *influence* on the stakeholders
- Their *relationship* with you

Ultimately, you want each team member to become an active 'change champion' but some stakeholders will be more amenable to this than others and timing is of the essence as you can only make each intervention once.

Each intervention can impact an individual's relationship with you and their adoption of the proposed change, or both of these. Players need to decide which intervention is optimum for each individual during each round.

As well as intervening with individuals, players can also intervene with teams and the group of 10 stakeholders as a whole. This is used to highlight the power of peer influence in gaining support from an individual. For example, an individual might be personally opposing a change and so having a group intervention with them and two supporting colleagues might be more fruitful than just having a one-to-one.

Briefing materials, in the forms of bios, are also provided for each of the 10 directors in the organisation. There are two types of bios – public bios (which are freely available to everyone) and private bios (which are only discovered after you begin to engage with a specific individual). There is also an organisation chart which indicates the organisational influence and a social network which represents the social influence in terms of the relationships, reputations and social interactions at work.

The simulation uses agent-based techniques so that any time an individual is influenced, there is an impact on all the other individuals, depending on their organisational and social influence.

The briefing materials provide the necessary information to determine the required change management intervention per individual, team or whole group. The simulation uses the latest experiential and social learning techniques to amplify the learning. Simulations typically run for half a day with 3-4 teams, each with 4-6 players.

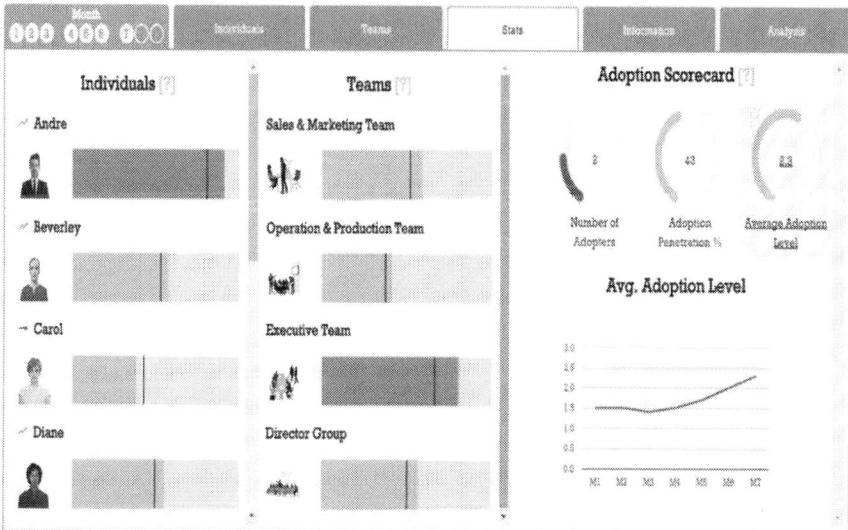

14.3.2 – COHORT Results Screen

More details on COHORT can be found at:
www.dashboardsimulations.com

14.4 CREW Work & Team Management Simulation

The CREW Simulation is an online simulation which allows project managers and prospective project managers to experience some of the challenges in *leading* a High Performing Team. CREW is complementary to CHAPTER (described in 14.6) but is more about leading and managing such a team effectively on an on-going basis.

CREW is very popular with medium/large organisations as it powerfully demonstrates the dramatic difference in results between managers who merely schedule their colleagues to work versus those managers who also recognise the importance of managing their colleagues as real people with motivations, skills, ambitions and challenges.

The scenario in CREW is that you have five colleagues in your team and you must manage their workload, personal, team and any project issues which occur in a four-week period. It is played in a half day simulation session.

It's a very hands-on role and the job is to resource important tasks in the most effective way by scheduling resources to work tasks. Each colleague has different levels of skills and motivations. Also, the relationship and influence of the team manager on each colleague is uniquely different. The work tasks differ in four important aspects:

- Urgency
- Priority
- Size
- Complexity

The main CREW decisions screen is shown in figure 14.4.1:

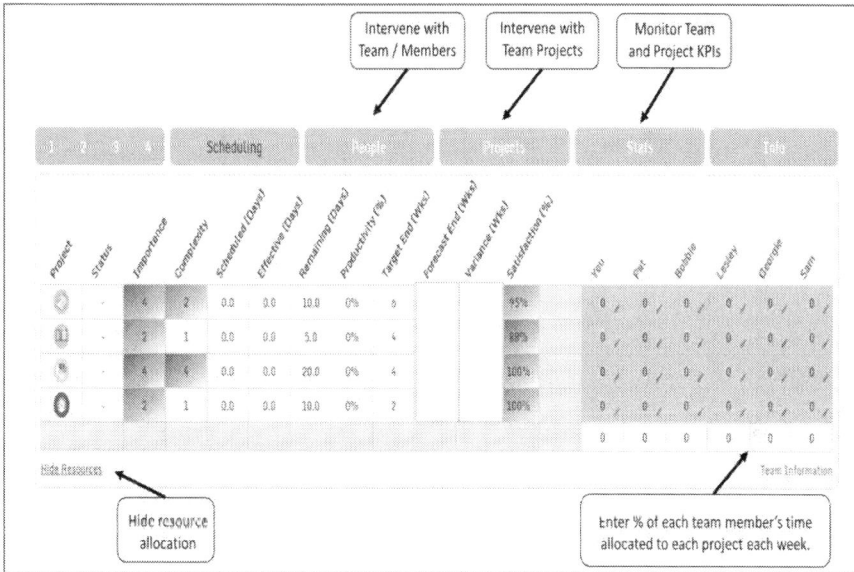

14.4.1 – Main CREW Simulation Screen

Figure 14.4.2 is the main CREW results tracking screen which allows participants to actively monitor and effectively react to results and trends in four key areas of team management:

- Project Schedules
- Business Value and Customer Satisfaction Levels
- Team Management
- Staff Management (Capabilities, Motivation, Well-being and Relationships)

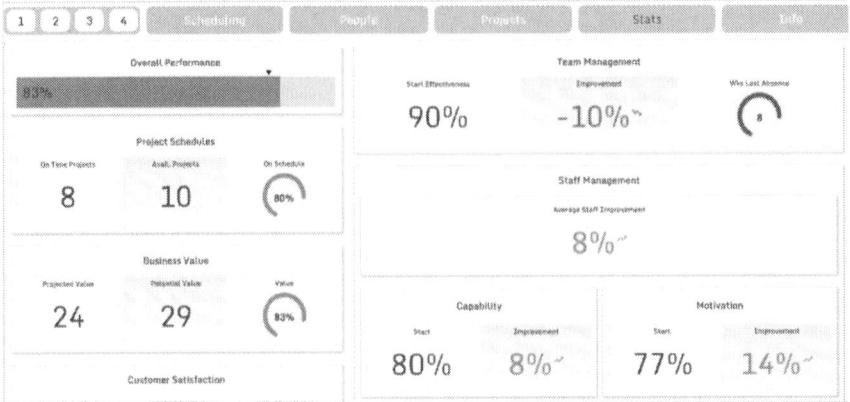

14.4.2 – Main CREW Results Screen

More details on CREW can be found at:
www.dashboardsimulations.com

14.5 SPREAD Project Roll-out Simulation

SPREAD is a computer-based business simulation which provides a 'what-if' planning capability for any change which involves rolling out a new practice or innovation to a well-defined community using *one-to-many* interventions.

Specifically, the simulation allows leaders and managers to explore the effectiveness and sequencing of different types of *one-to-many* interventions and attempt to move a whole community from 'unaware' to 'fully adopted'.

In technical terms, SPREAD is a Change Diffusion Model.

It can be customised for the organisation, change and target community, and therefore can be used as a management tool to 'test and tune' the planning of a mass change. For example, it has been used in healthcare to model the roll-out of new healthcare practices ('the innovation') within defined practitioner groups ('the target community').

It can also be played as a team game to educate players about the change and to develop wider ownership of the change across a change leadership team.

A typical SPREAD simulation includes a New Product Launch within external customer communities or a New Strategy / Process / Behaviour Roll-out within internal organisational communities.

After a group has played SPREAD to prepare for an upcoming major change rollout, they will have a much clearer understanding of what is really involved. They will be much better equipped to envisage the change, plan it, identify the key risks and manage more effectively when the unexpected happens - because they have already simulated it!

SPREAD can be configured with any of the tasks required for a rollout and all team decisions are saved and can be "action-replayed" afterwards, to deepen the learning.

Results are shown graphically using high impact charts that reflect user adoption, budget spend, user benefits and other key roll-out measures.

Figure 14.5.1 summarises the different type of initiatives which can be applied to a community change using SPREAD.

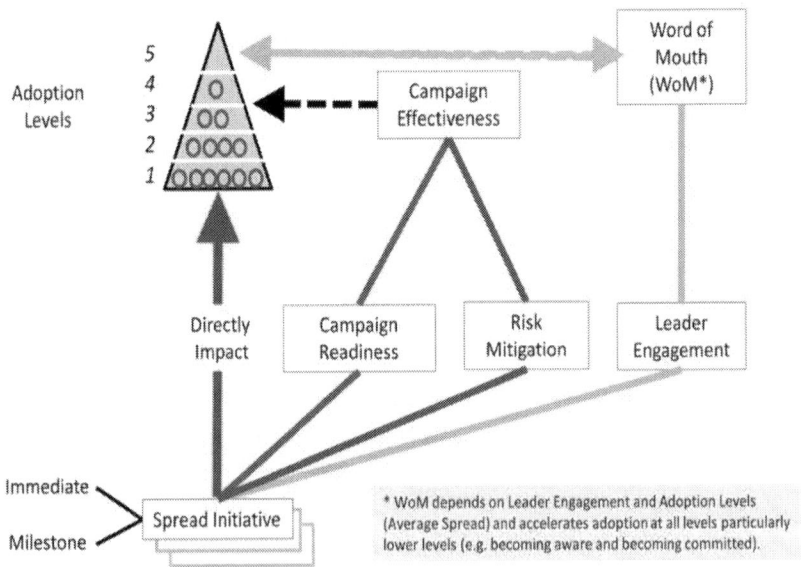

Figure 14.5.1 - Different Types of SPREAD Initiative

Figure 14.5.2 has been taken from a typical SPREAD session. On the left there is a list of possible SPREAD initiatives and their status. The four gauges graphically depict the progress made on Readiness, Leader Engagement, Milestones and Adoption.

The charts and the table to the right show how user adoption is moving through the different stages - from Unaware right the way through to Sustaining.

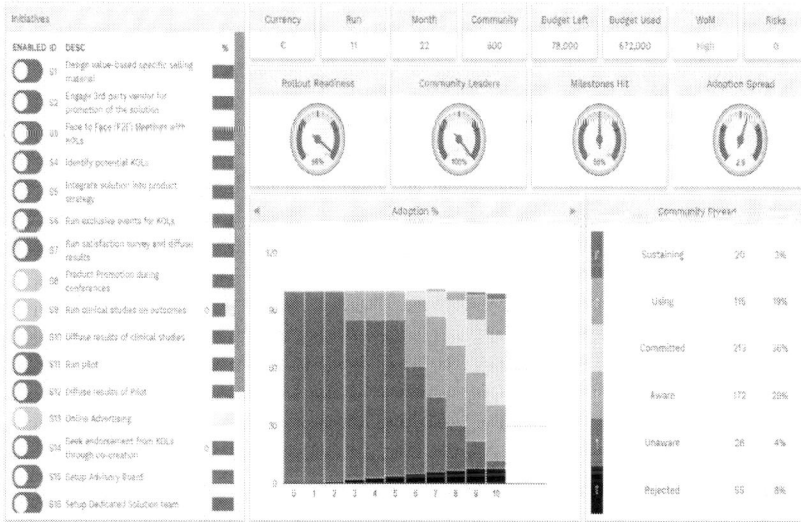

Figure 14.5.2 - Main SPREAD Screen

SPREAD can be configured for any number of initiatives which may be required for a specific roll-out programme.

For example:

- One-off Initiatives or Repeatable for a maximum number of times
- Single or multiple periods to complete (Milestones)

- Initiatives which depend on other activities completing before they can commence
- Initiatives which can be repeated but with a time delay between them

Each SPREAD initiative can have any or all off the following characteristics:

- It enhances the readiness of the Rollout Campaign and the effectiveness of all subsequent initiatives
- It engages the Community Leaders to promote 'Word of Mouth' viral adoption
- It mitigates against future risks to the rollout
- It directly enables users to move up a level of adoption on a five-point scale

More details on SPREAD can be found at: www.dashboardsimulations.com

14.6 CHAPTER Team Formation Simulation

The CHAPTER Simulation covers both the process and change aspects of developing an effective team. It allows prospective team leaders and project managers to practice their team-building skills in a safe environment. Figures 14.6.1 and 14.6.2 show how players have the opportunity to try out all of the change management and process development interventions discussed in Chapter 11, with a newly formed team of 10 members.

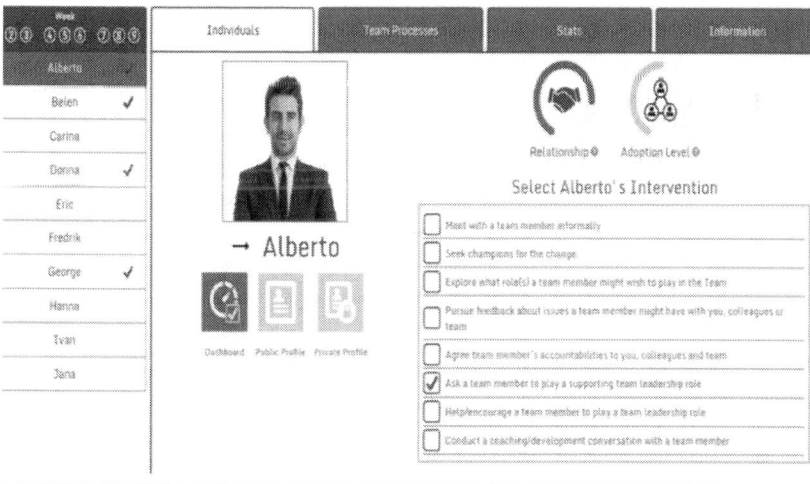

Figure 14.6.1 - CHAPTER Individual Decisions Screen

Players must choose carefully which interventions to make with each team member considering three key factors:

- Their *attitude* to the idea of the high performing team
- Their *influence* on the other team members
- Their *relationship* with you

Ultimately you want each team member to play a supporting leadership role in the team but certain team members will be more amenable to this than others and timing is everything as you can only make each intervention once.

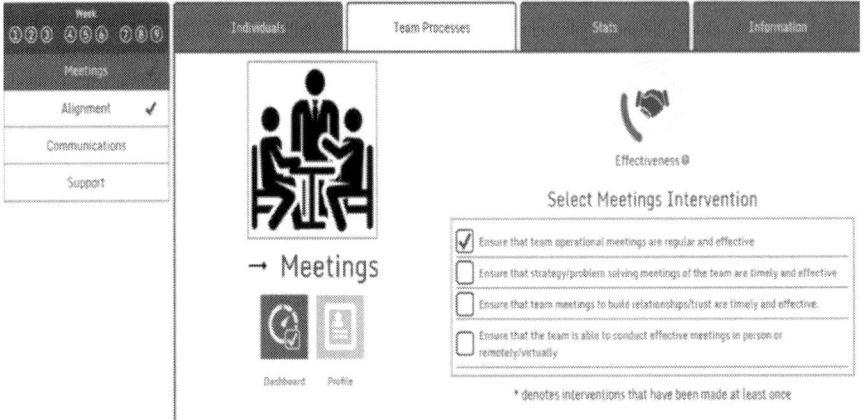

Figure 14.6.2 - CHAPTER Process Decisions Screen

As well as intervening with individuals, players must also intervene to fix (or create) the necessary key processes and practices to operate as a high performing team in four important areas:

- Meetings
- Alignment and Accountability
- Communications
- Support

As part of the simulation, the players must analyse the briefing material on the fictitious company. Briefing materials, in the forms of bios, are also provided for each team member along with a team organisation chart and social network.

The briefing materials provide the necessary information to determine the required change management intervention per individual and allow the players to conduct an initial Health Check on the team as a whole.

The simulation itself is played in teams and uses the latest experiential and social learning techniques to amplify the learning. Simulations typically run for half a day with 3-4 teams, each of 4-6 players.

More details on CHAPTER can be found at:
www.dashboardsimulations.com

APPENDICES

Appendix A: Project Management Tasks Infographic

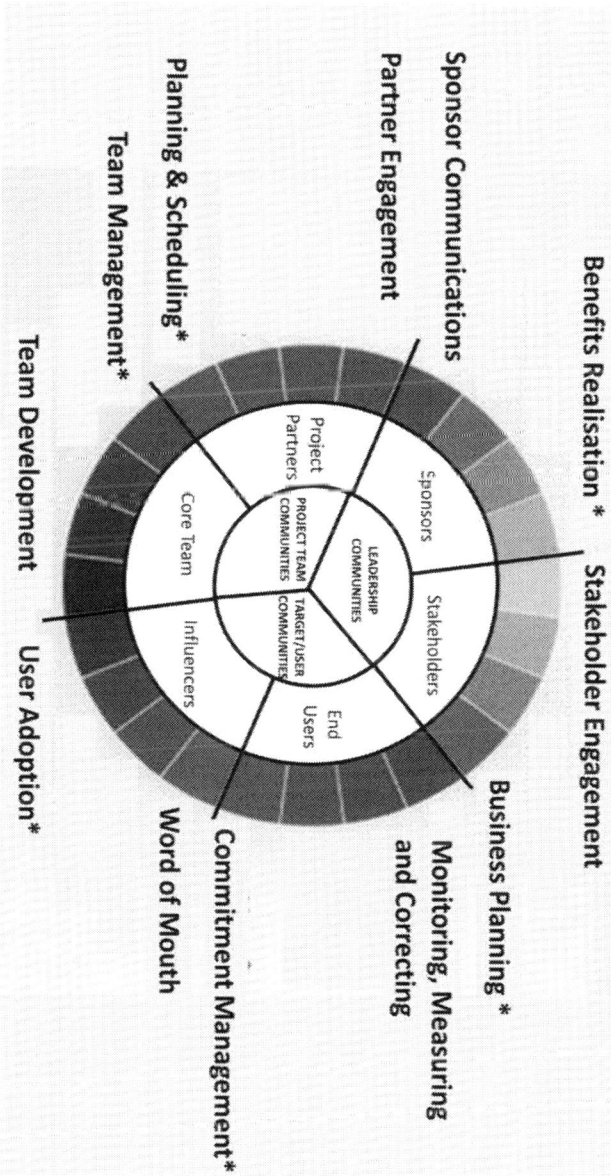

Appendix B: Project Manager's Jobs Infographic

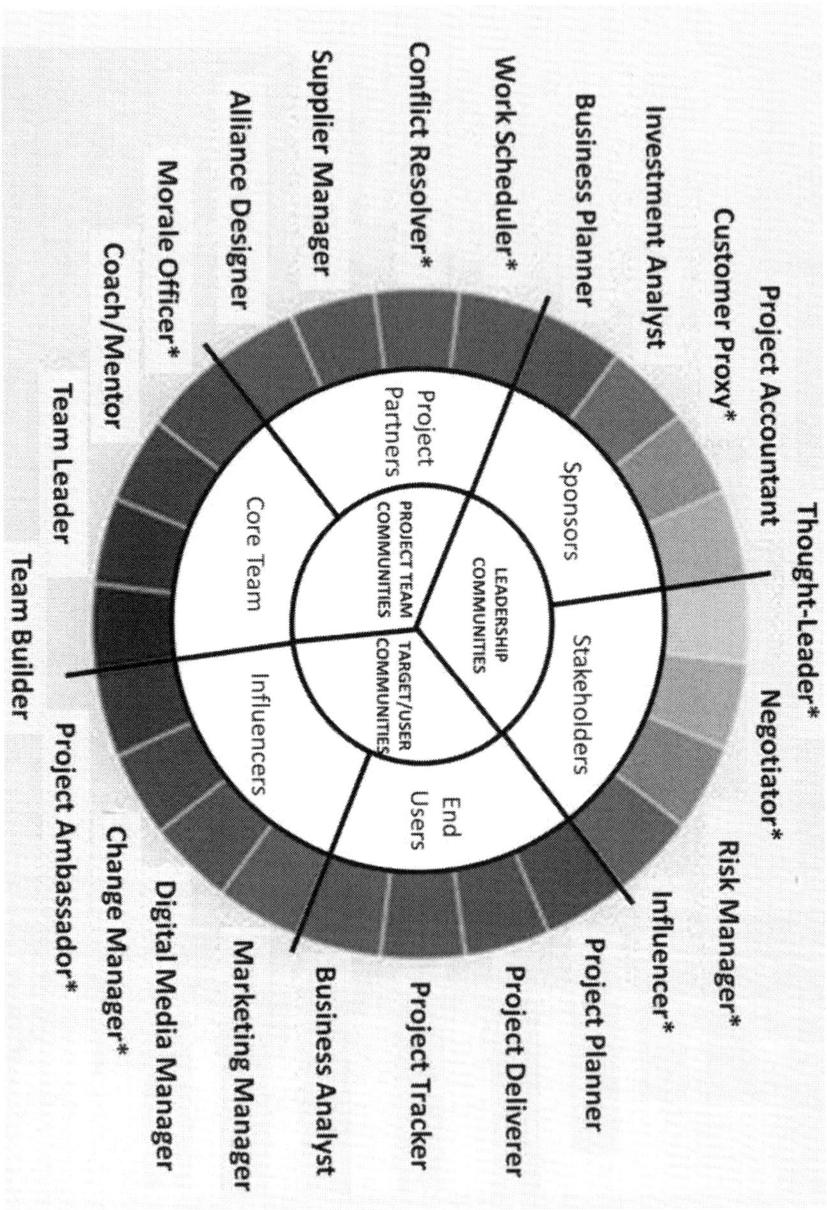
Thought-Leader*
Project Accountant
Customer Proxy*
Investment Analyst
Business Planner
Work Scheduler*
Conflict Resolver*
Supplier Manager
Alliance Designer
Morale Officer*
Coach/Mentor
Team Leader
Team Builder
Project Ambassador*
Change Manager*
Digital Media Manager
Marketing Manager
Business Analyst
Project Tracker
Project Deliverer
Project Planner
Influencer*
Risk Manager*
Negotiator*
Sponsors
Stakeholders
End Users
Influencers
Core Team
Project Partners
LEADERSHIP COMMUNITIES
PROJECT TEAM COMMUNITIES
TARGET/USER COMMUNITIES

Appendix C: High Speed Project Teams

Can you create a High-Performing Team in a day or in an afternoon or even over lunch? Of course not! However, if you are put in the position where you, as a leader, must get the very best out of a group of colleagues in very short timescales, then what can you do?

Here is our four-step approach to 'Instant Team'.

STEP1: Create Team 'Game Plan'

Here is a seven-point checklist which teams can use to produce a Team Game Plan (1-2 pages maximum):

1. **R**oles

How will we divide up the team responsibilities?

2. **A**greements (Ground Rules)

How will we deal with each other as colleagues and team members?

3. **P**rocesses/Practices

What are the 2-3 most important team processes/practices that we will put in place and follow?

4. **P**riorities

How will we decide what is most important, particularly in dilemmas or when under pressure?

5. **O**rganisational Values

What values are the most important to us as a team?

6.   Results

What specific results must we achieve as our minimum team performance level?

7.   Targets

What is our 'stretch' target i.e., our ambition to exceed the minimum performance level?

The first letter of each element spells 'RAPPORT', which is a useful mnemonic for a Team Game Plan. This is apt, as 'Rapport' can be defined as:

'A close and harmonious relationship in which the groups concerned understand each other's feelings or ideas and communicate well.' Source: The Oxford Dictionary.

STEP 2: Test the Team

Conduct a short team-based activity and try to follow your Team Game Plan. You need to set aside at least one hour but three hours is better as you can play a team-based business simulation or even some off-site activity. If you only have an hour, you can still have a team problem-solving and brainstorming meeting on a practical topic that everyone is familiar with.

STEP 3: Reflect and Improve

At the end of this activity, team members should take at least 30 minutes to discuss and reflect on a small number of key questions typically:

- How well are we working as a team – what could we improve?
- What would we do differently if we performed the activity again?

- How closely are we following our team game plan – does this need to be revised?

If you have the three hours, then you can conduct this review more than once as this allows the team to see visible improvements quickly. Another very useful device is to have the teams perform a self-assessment against the *'7 Mistakes teams make under pressure'*, depicted in Figure C.1.

These findings have been gathered over the last 10 years and represent the most common mistakes teams make when participating in team-based business simulation games.

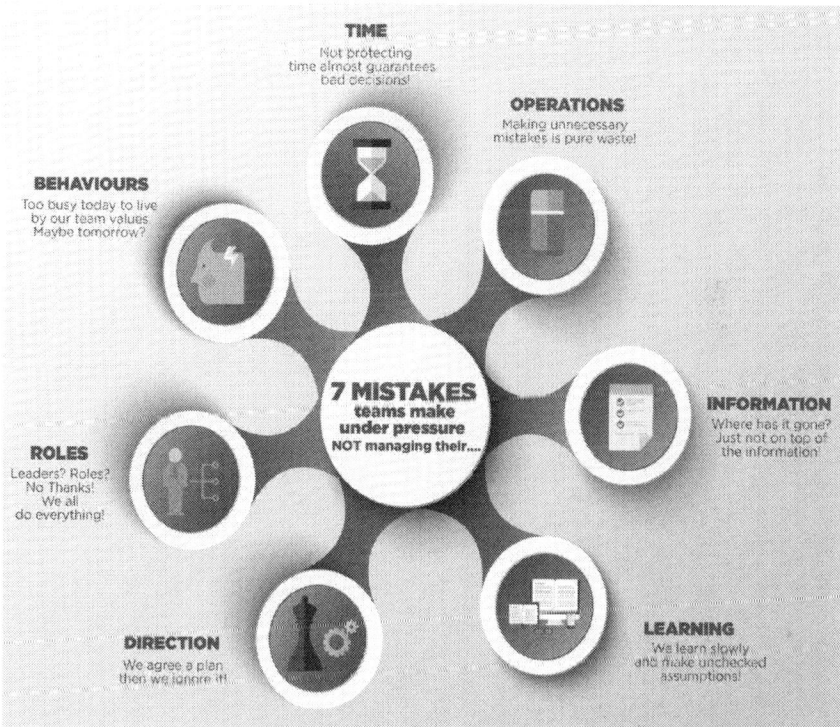

Figure C.1 – '7 Mistakes teams make under pressure'

STEP 4: Execute and Review

Now you need to direct the team to the job in hand with the specific extra directive of 'Follow your Game Plan!' In addition, you must build in a regular (e.g., weekly) review cycle where you repeat the self-reflection/improvement from Step 3 using, of course, all the other guidance and tools offered earlier in this book!

The Evolution of Team Working

If you observe newly-formed and existing teams playing business simulations and other intensive challenges, you can gain some important insights into how team-working 'evolves'. This knowledge can help you to accelerate the evolution of effective team working and collaboration in your own organisational teams.

On the road to Effective Team Collaboration, there seems to be two intermediate phases of 'naïve collaboration' which teams often seem to go through - *Hyper-Communication* and *Over-Delegation. (See Figure C.2)*

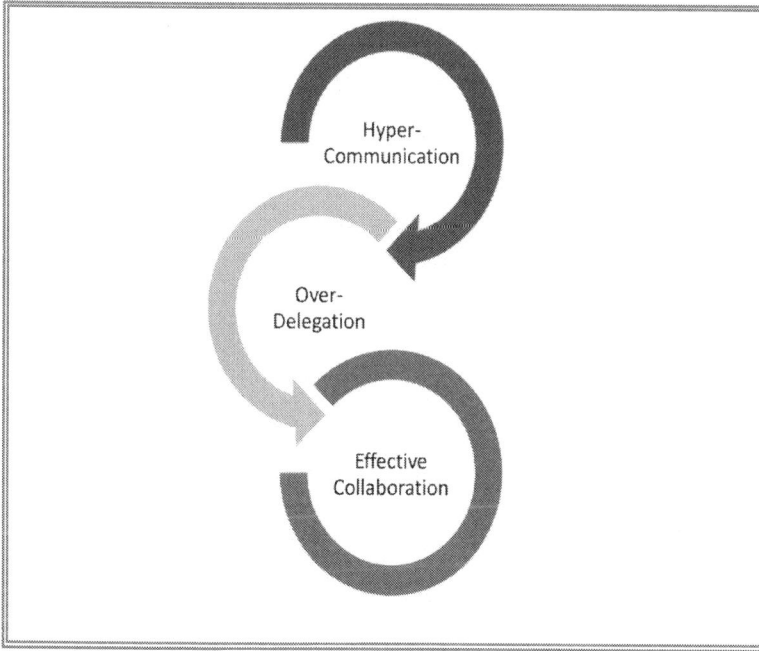

Figure C.2 - The Evolution of Effective Team-working

PHASE 1: Hyper-Communication

In this phase, almost every team member is involved in virtually every single team conversation. It is very democratic and feels good but the problem is that it just takes forever. A team operating like this will not hit its deadlines.

An organisational team meeting which conducts its Operational Meetings like this will not get through its agenda.

In our experience, teams usually start here on their journey towards effective collaboration. Teams in this phase genuinely believe that they are collaborating well

UNTIL they suddenly discover that working like this is just not practical as it simply takes too long!

When teams have tried 'Hyper-Communication', they often *over-correct* and move to the next phase of naive collaboration - 'Over-Delegation'.

PHASE 2: Over-Delegation

In this phase, the team quickly agree that they need to work faster and more efficiently. To achieve this, they wisely decide that they need some roles and a division of labour but then 'over-delegate'. In other words, they tend to give out jobs to the different members and sub-teams but do not support this with sufficient communications to ensure they all stay on the same page.

Like the first phase, Hyper-Communication, teams think they have fixed their collaboration problem and feel they are being very efficient UNTIL they discover, typically near the end of the round, that they are no longer all on the same page and that the team members have been working to different assumptions and priorities. This invalidates much of their good work.

PHASE 3: Effective Collaboration

Once the teams have experienced both naïve forms of collaboration (Hyper-Communication and Over-Delegation), they are well placed to find a middle ground which represents Effective Collaboration.

As with Over-Delegation, they allocate roles but this time they also ensure that this is supported by on-going communications particularly around task objectives and early review of provisional findings/decisions before they become finalised.

Accelerated Team Development

From these insights, most teams find it very difficult to move directly into Effective Collaboration without first experiencing **and learning** from both Hyper-Communication and Over-Delegation.

Although there is no evidence, we feel strongly that it may be the case that many organisational teams simply *flip-flop* between the two naïve collaboration phases of Hyper-Communication and Over-Delegation without ever making the break-through into Effective Collaboration - perhaps believing all the time that they are already doing it!

Therefore, to fast track effective team-working, you need three simple ingredients:

1. **Mechanisms such as competitive business simulation games** or other short team challenges.

2. **Briefing for the teams on the challenges with specific deadlines and goals** but without any instruction about how they are to behave other than that they are a team.

3. **Facilitated team self-analysis sessions at the end of each round** or chunk of work, to let the teams review what kind of collaboration they are employing and how they might improve it.

If you carefully and skilfully work with these three ingredients, you can help teams in your organisation to develop effective team-working and collaboration skills in a much faster timescale than might be possible using other methods. *This appendix is a short extract from book 1 in The Systematic Guide series: 'A Systematic Guide to High Performing Teams (HPTs).*

Appendix D: Key Principles of Change Management

In Ken's book "A Systematic Guide to Change Management", he identifies 12 core principles which underpin successful change management implementations. It is always useful to keep these in mind at all times. They serve as a useful antidote to overly prescriptive change management approaches.

1. What is the Story of the Change?

2. Have a Change Plan

3. Never fly blind

4. Measure twice — cut once

5. Round up your supporters

6. But don't ignore powerful opponents

7. Influence the Influential

8. If you can't be direct, then be indirect

9. Don't forget those who helped get you started

10. Rome was not built in a day

11. Expect unexpected Change

12. Finally, rip up that Change cookbook

Further Reading

For a more detailed exploration of change management and influencing see "A Systematic Guide to Change Management" by Ken Thompson, July 2016.

Appendix E: Developing Coaching Relationships

In his exceptional book, *Coaching – Evoking Excellence in Others,* James Flaherty suggests that 'interventions in competence to improve the actions of others' should only be called 'coaching' if they adhere to the following five operating principles:

1.   Relationship
Based on a relationship of mutual respect, mutual trust and freedom of expression.

2.   Pragmatism
Based not on abstract theory but on the principle that 'what is true is what works'.

3.   Two Tracks
An engaged learning experience for both the client and the coach.

4.   Always/Already
Respectful that those being coached are not empty vessels and bring with them their own unique life experiences and ways of dealing with things.

5.   Techniques don't work
Not reliant on selecting the right coaching 'techniques' as a substitute for the absence of any of the other four operating principles.

There are many different approaches you can use for coaching. The most important thing is that you use something that feels comfortable to you personally. Otherwise you run the risk of failing one of Flaherty's five coaching operating principles such as being too technique-oriented.

At the very simplest level, you might use 'Instant Payoff Coaching' described in *The Tao of Coaching*, by Max Landsberg, which can be summarised in four simple steps:

1. Define the Problem
2. Define the Ideal Outcome
3. Identify the Blocks (in the person being coached and elsewhere)
4. Brainstorm Solutions

This very simple coaching process also serves to illustrate two distinct development schools which coaches need to appreciate. By focusing on the problem and the blocks, we are employing what is known as a 'problem-based coaching' approach to personal development.

The alternative is a 'strengths-based' approach to coaching where an instant payoff coaching process might look more like this:

1. Agree some ambitions in an area
2. Take stock of where the person being coached has started and how far they have progressed
3. Identify the strengths and skills which enabled this
4. Brainstorm on how the person being coached could exploit these strengths to go even further

A good example of a 'strengths-based' coaching approach is described in the popular 2004 book *Now, Discover Your Strengths* by Marcus Buckingham.

'Problem-based' and 'Strengths-based' approaches both have their merits. It is, of course, entirely possible for a coach to use a 'hybrid approach' where they can draw from either depending on specific situations over the course of an on-going coaching relationship.

Mentoring: A Guide to the Basics by Gordon Shea (1992) suggests that 'A good mentor or coach will do one of the following things for you and, if you are lucky, a great one might do all three':

- Provide an "aha" experience
- Offer a saying or quote that helps you spot a behaviour to seek or avoid
- Help uncover an aspect or talent which until then had laid dormant.

Research by Jay Cross and published in his excellent book *Informal Learning* suggests that up to 95% of the skills people need to do their day-to-day jobs are not learned "formally" but "informally".

The three main techniques which constitute informal learning being:

1. Learning from your mistakes
2. Self-directed research/reading
3. Mentoring and coaching

Mentoring and coaching are not only vital components of informal learning in itself, they also underpin the other two techniques by helping people get a good perspective on their mistakes and pointing them at highly targeted reading materials.

INDEX

<u>Your Own Notes (1)</u>

Your Own Notes (2)

Your Own Notes (3)

<u>Your Own Notes (4)</u>

29552357R00115

Printed in Great Britain
by Amazon